ARE YOU
DISSING ME?

ARE YOU
DISSING ME?

WHAT ANIMALS
REALLY THINK

SIMON WINHELD

CHRONICLE BOOKS

SAN FRANCISCO

For Herschel

Library of Congress Cataloging-in-Publication Data available.
ISBN: 978-1-4521-3844-2

Manufactured in China

MIX
Paper from responsible sources
FSC® C008047

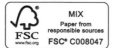

Designed by Neil Egan
Cover design assistance by Sally Carmichael

10 9 8 7 6 5 4 3 2 1

Chronicle Books LLC
680 Second Street
San Francisco, California 94107
www.chroniclebooks.com

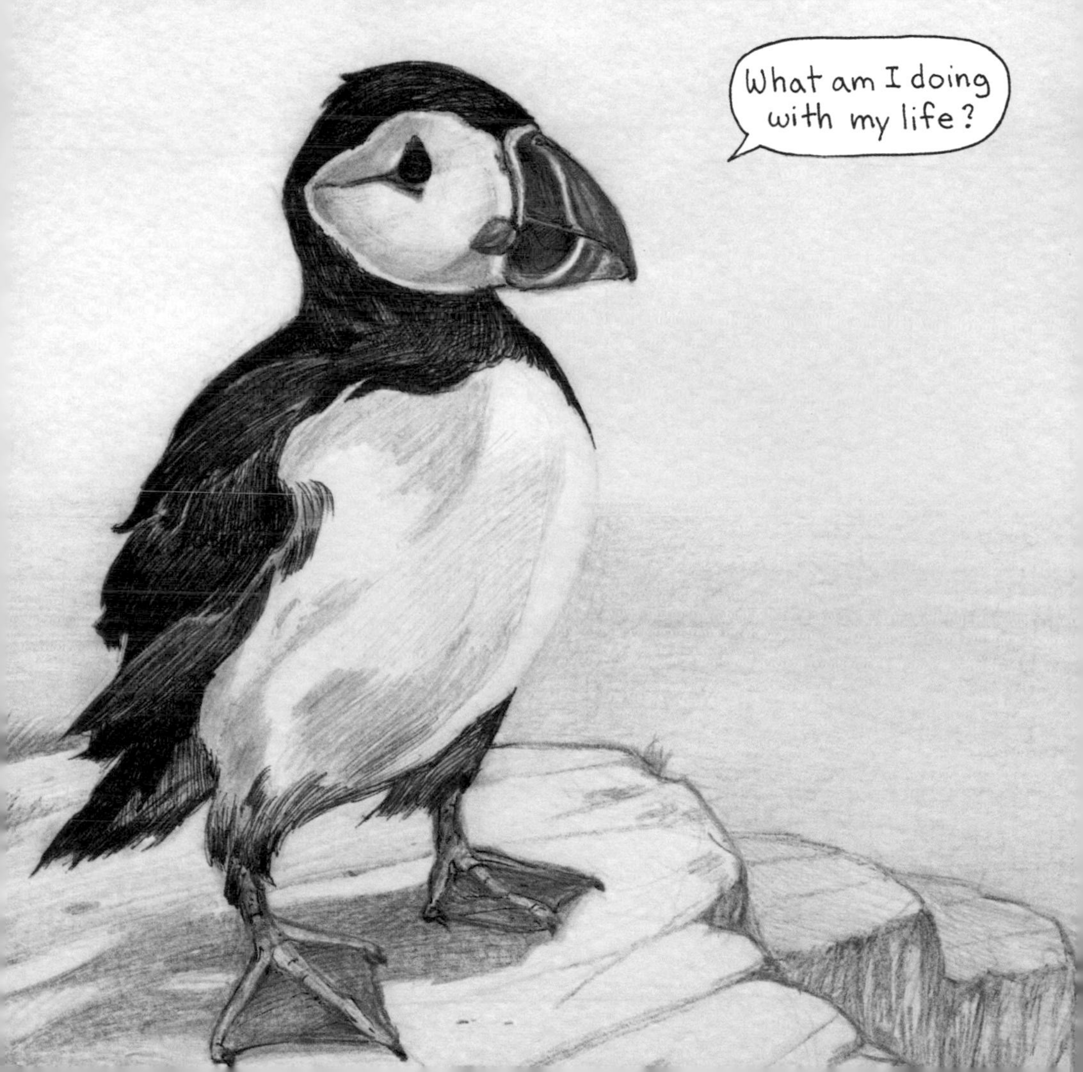
What am I doing with my life?

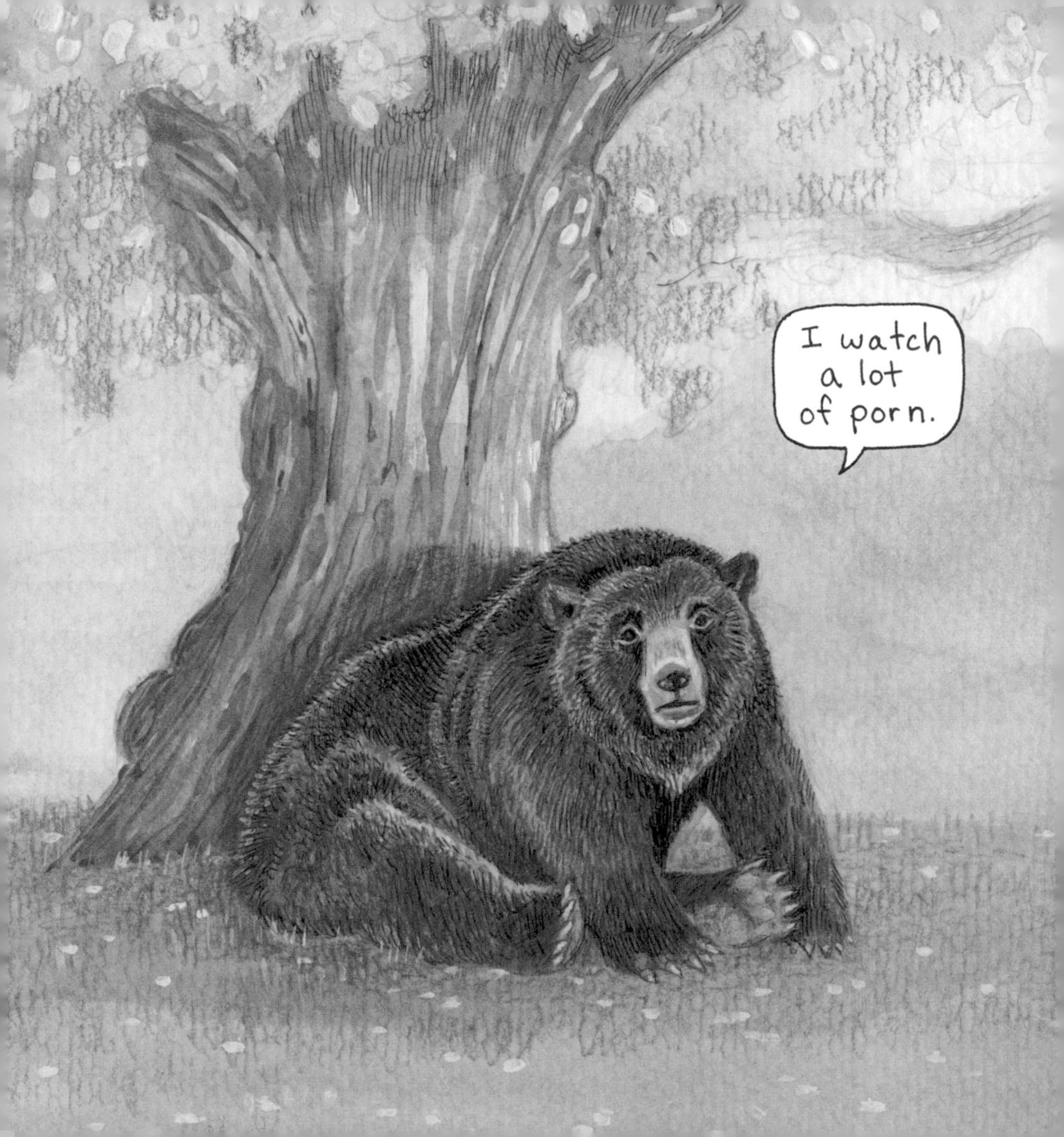
I watch a lot of porn.

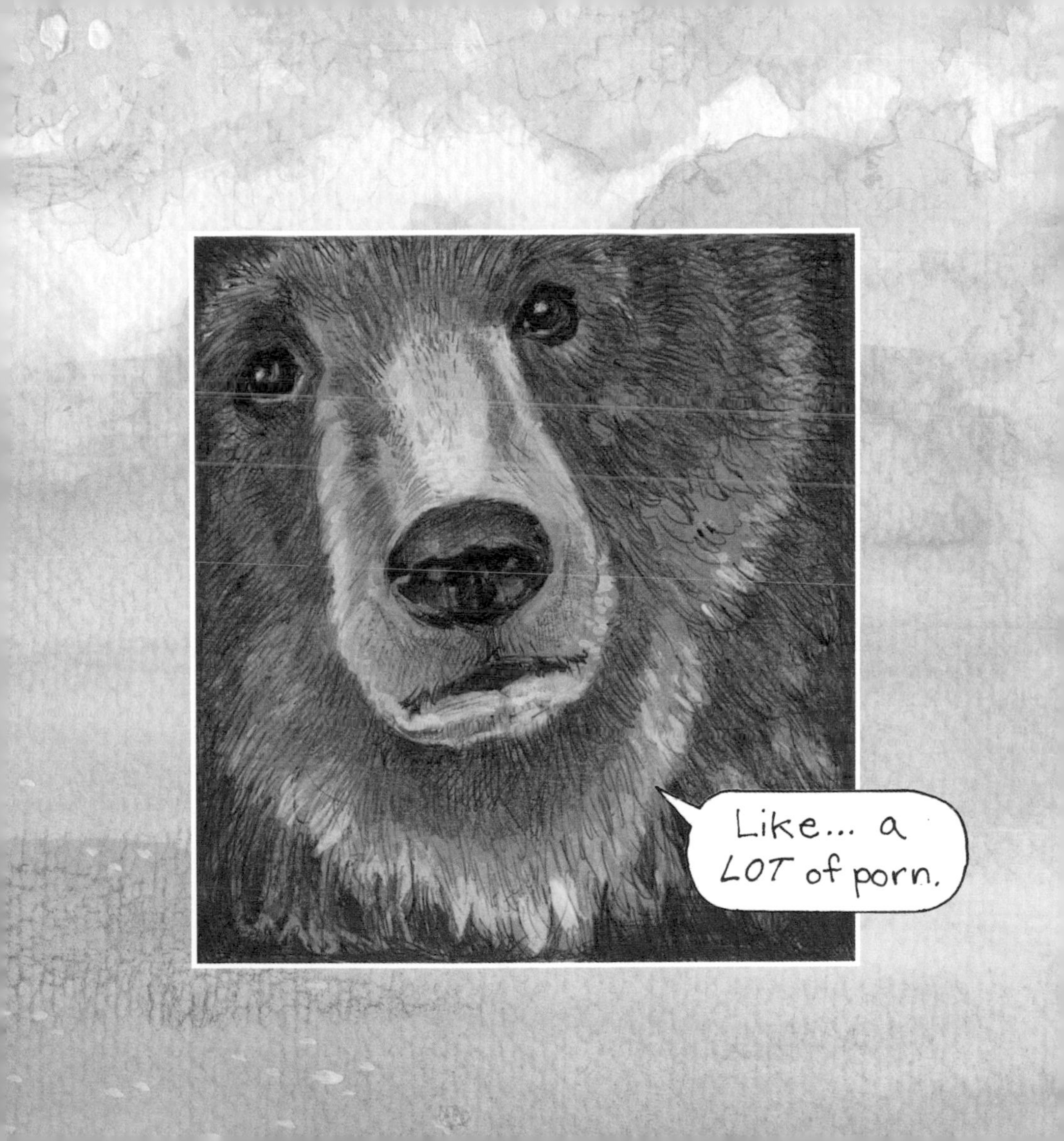
Like... a LOT of porn.

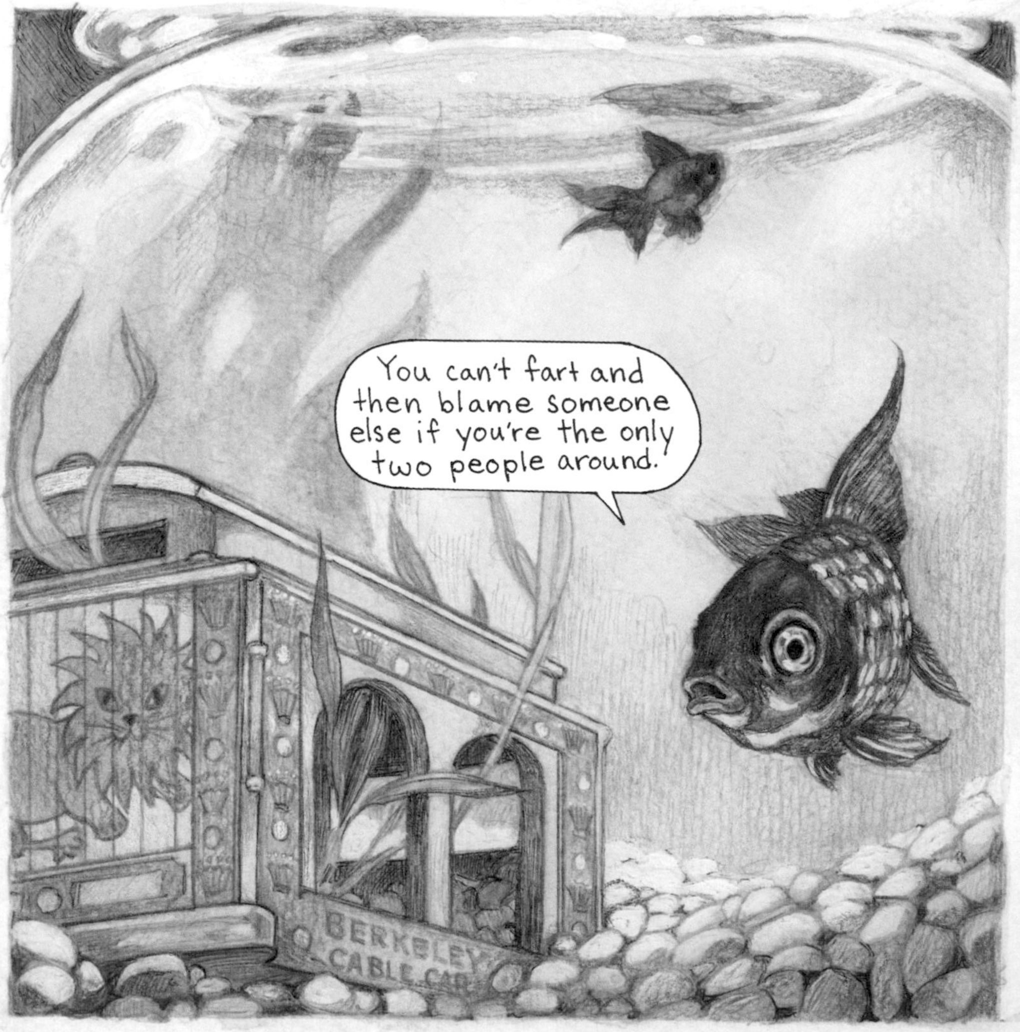
You can't fart and then blame someone else if you're the only two people around.
BERKELEY CABLE CAR

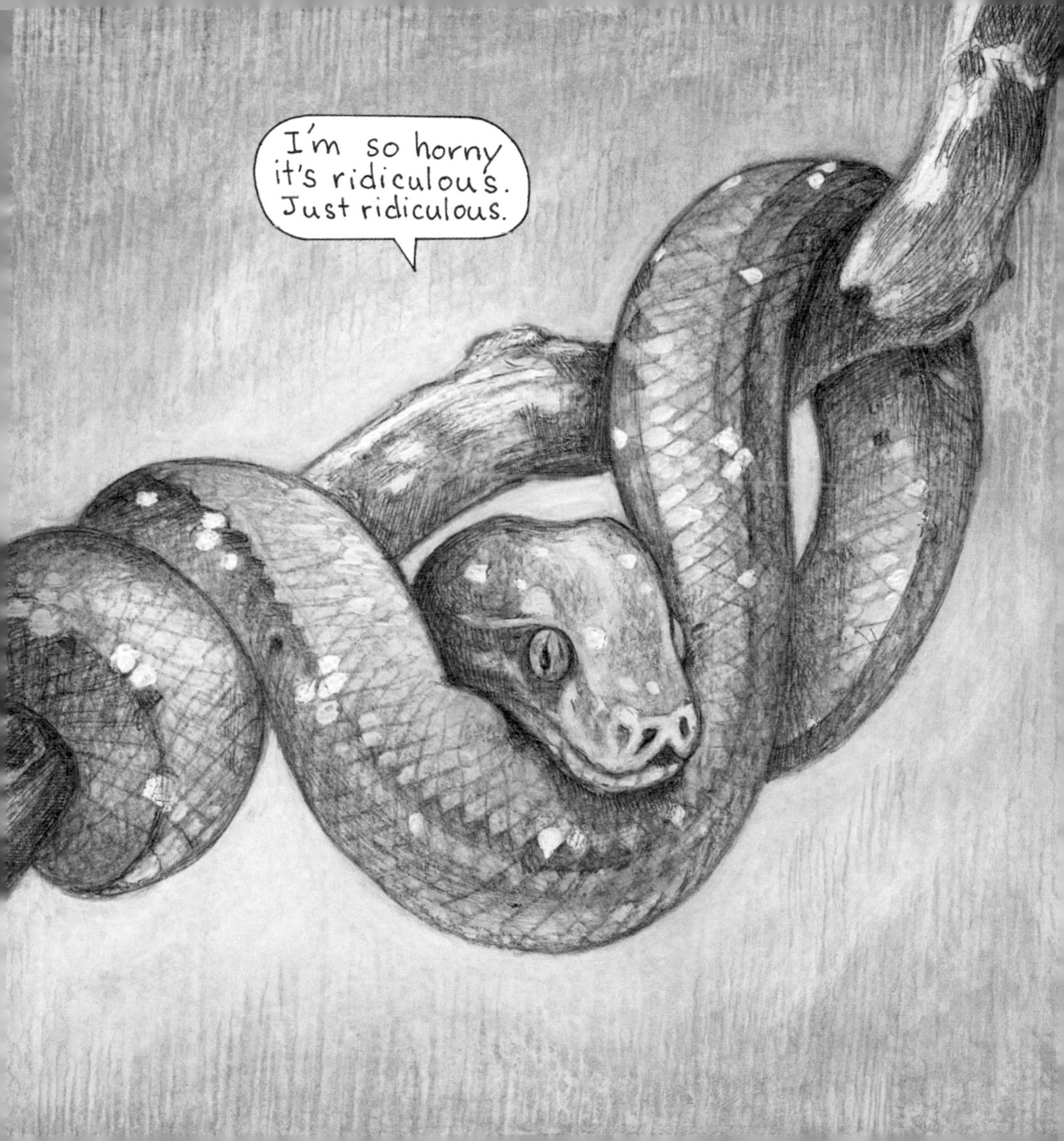
I'm so horny it's ridiculous. Just ridiculous.

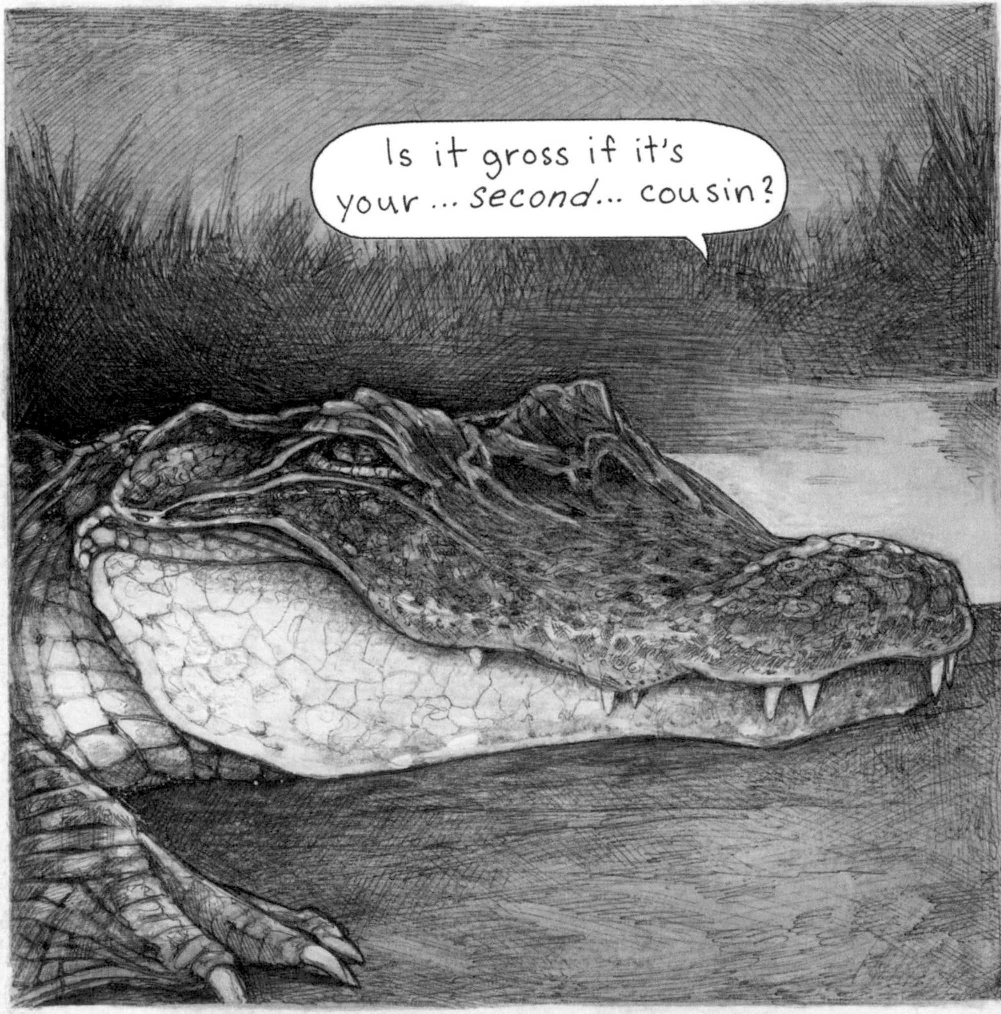
Is it gross if it's your ... second... cousin?

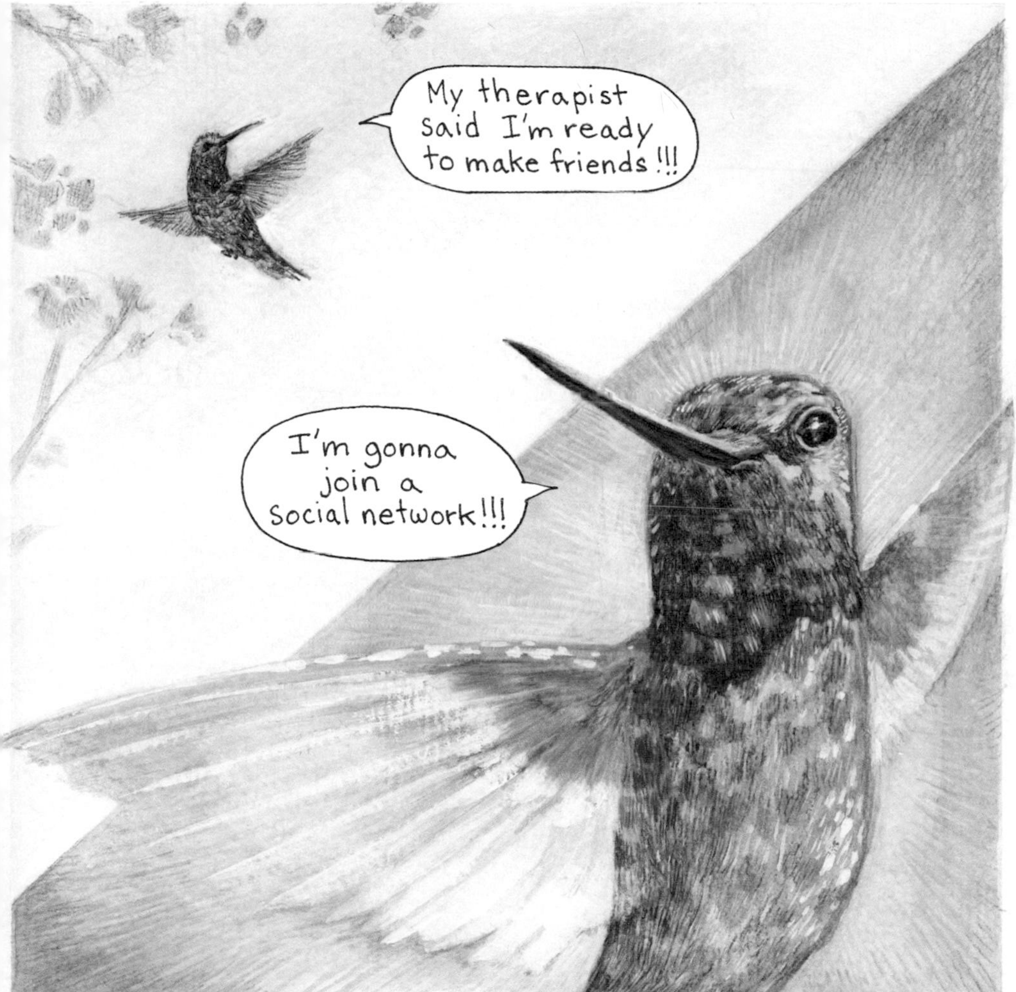
My therapist said I'm ready to make friends!!!
I'm gonna join a social network!!!

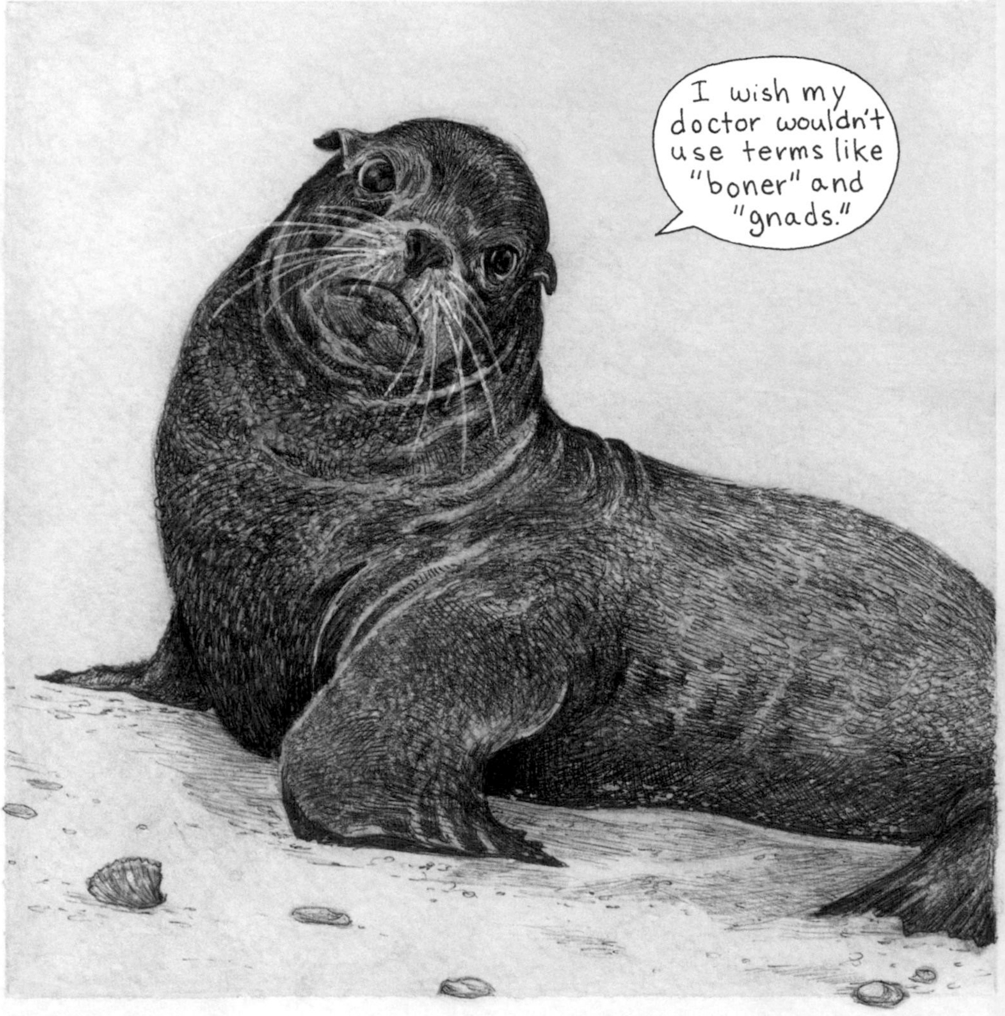
I wish my doctor wouldn't use terms like "boner" and "gnads."

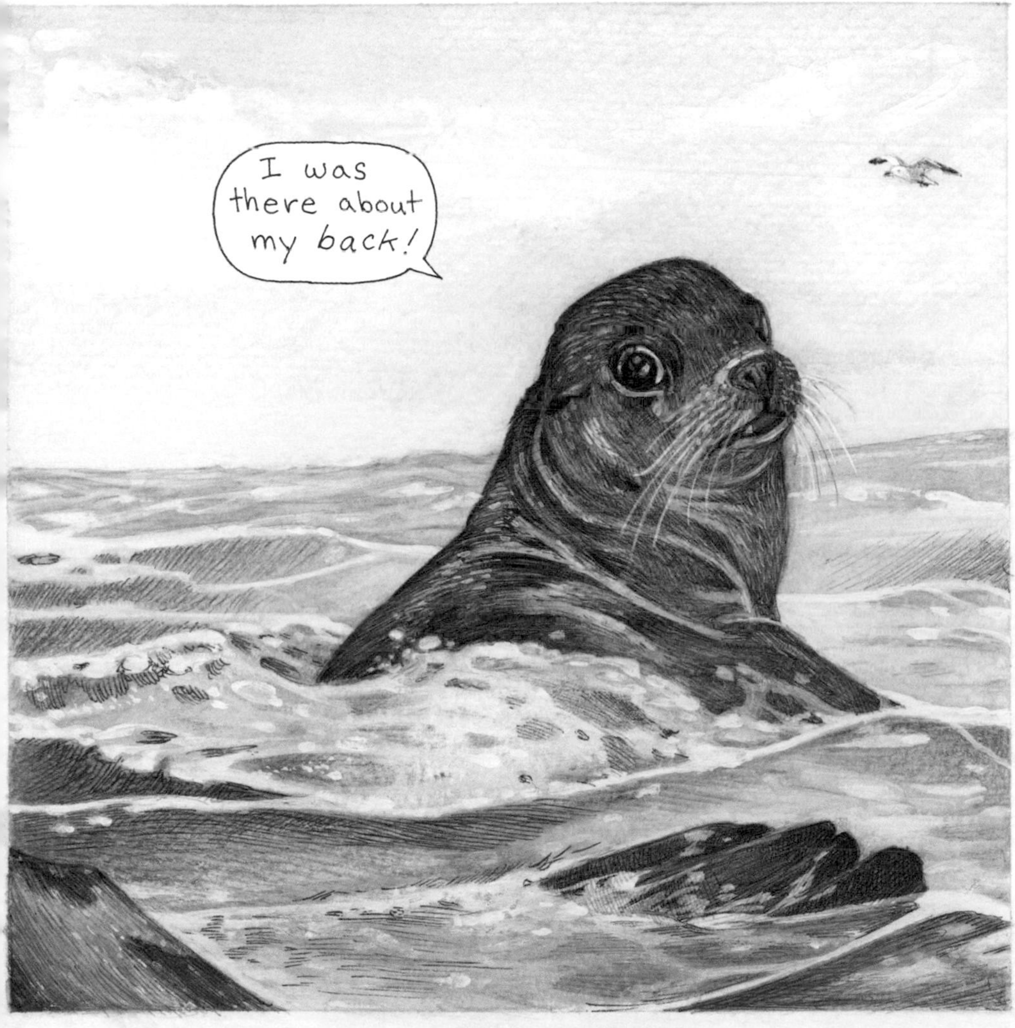
I was there about my back!

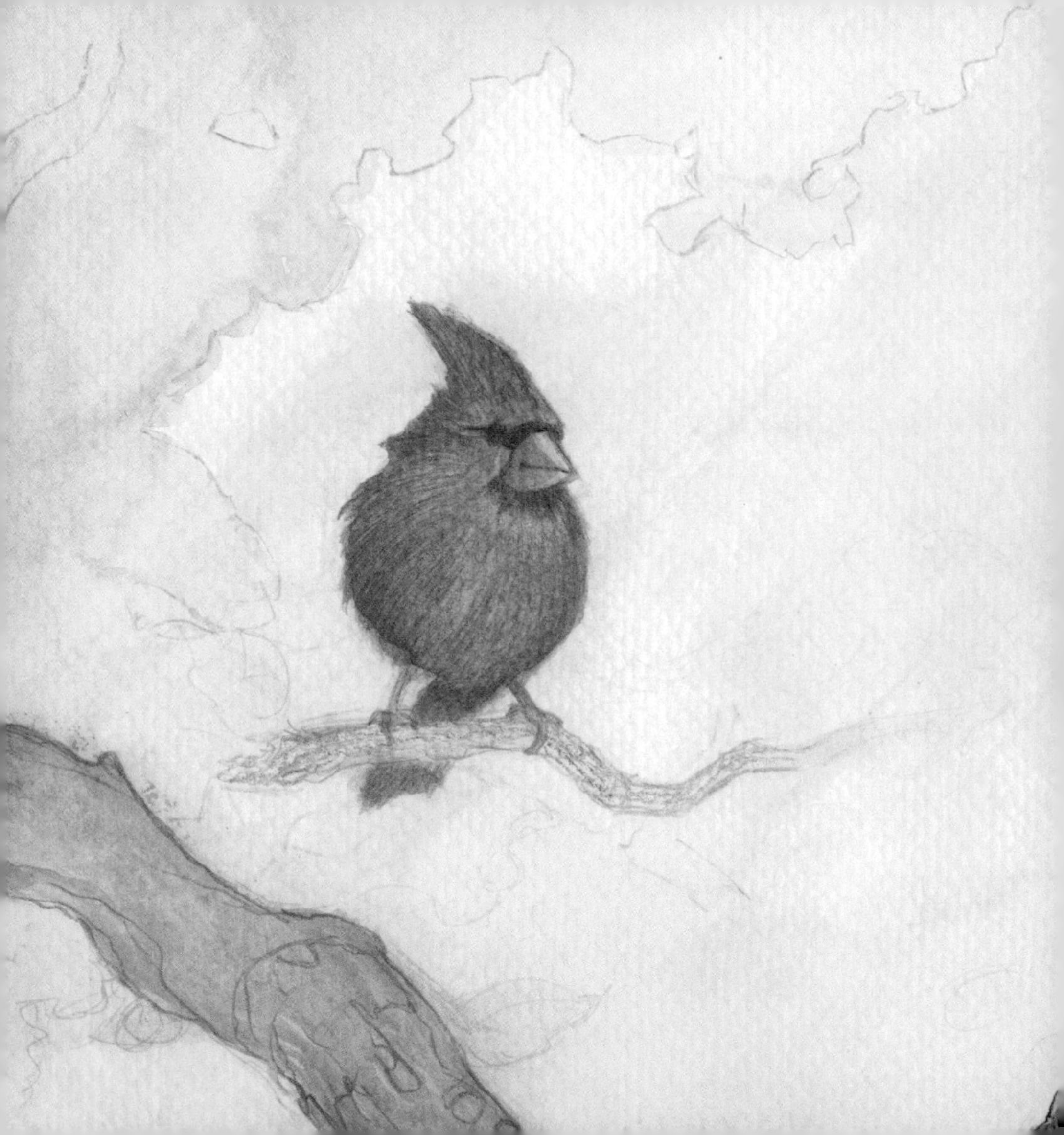

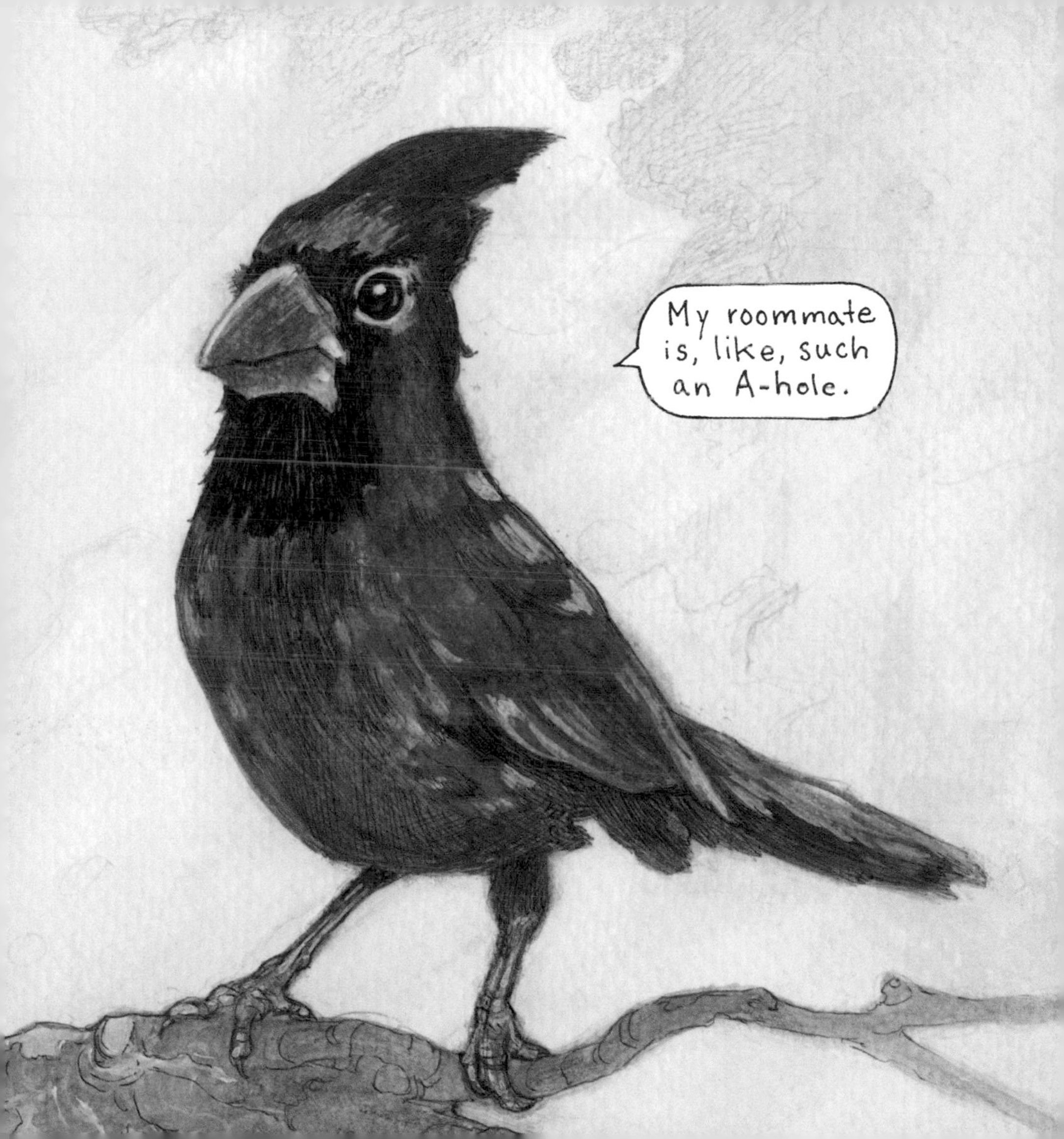
My roommate is, like, such an A-hole.

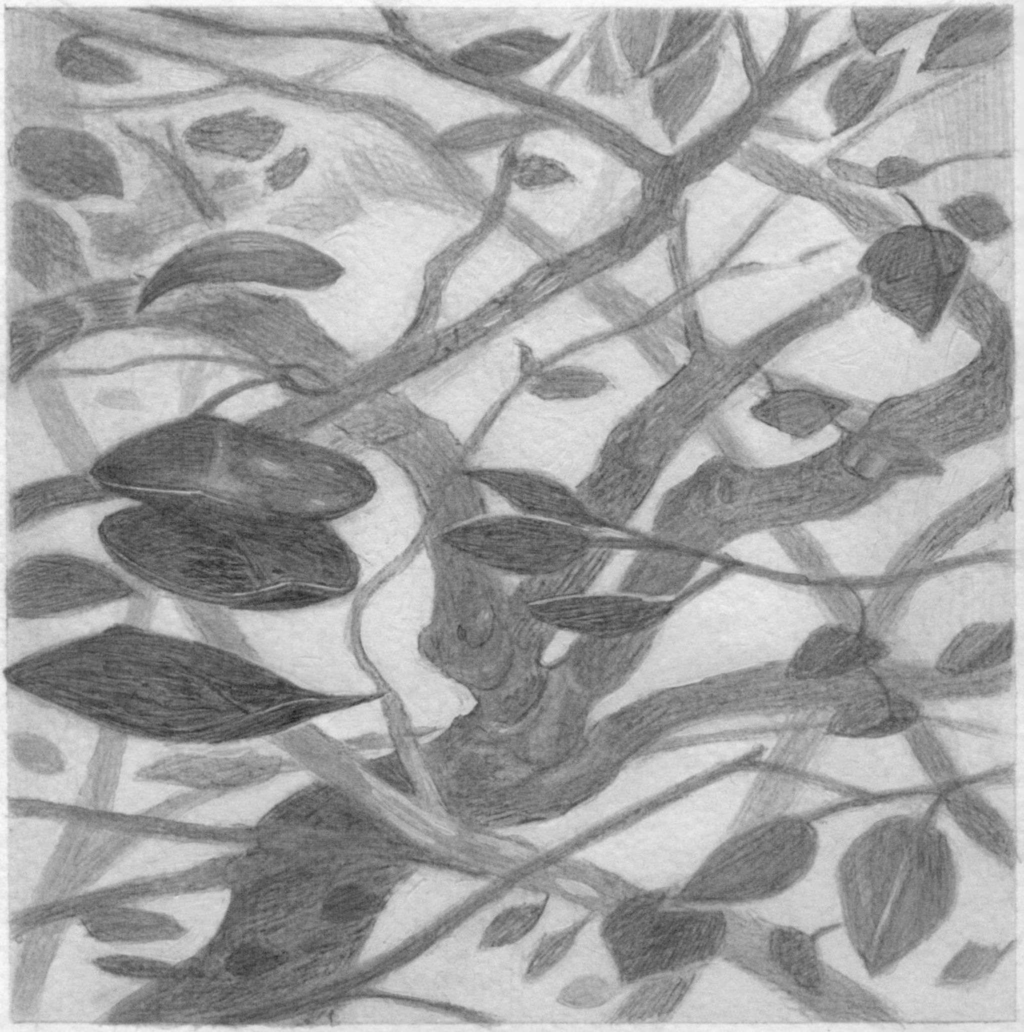

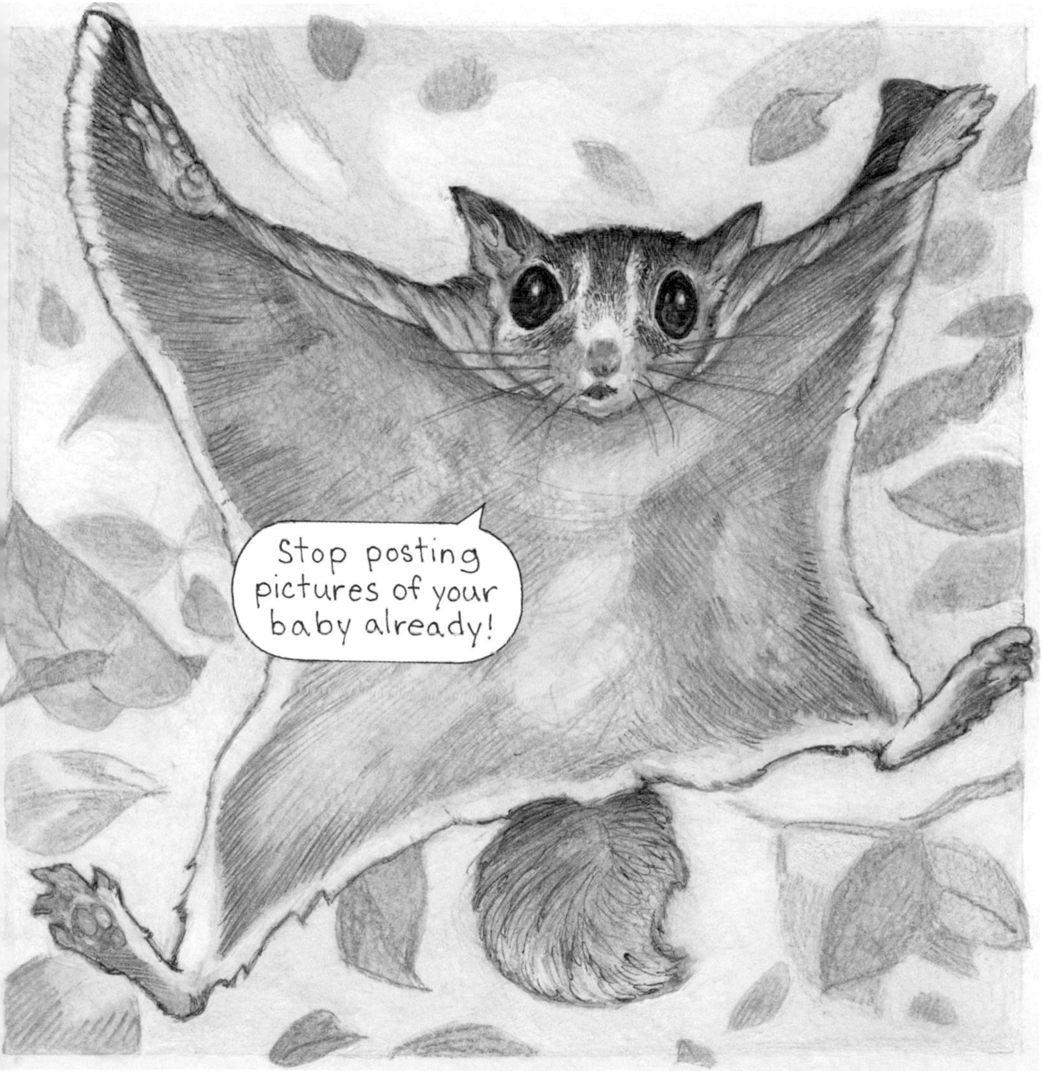
Stop posting pictures of your baby already!

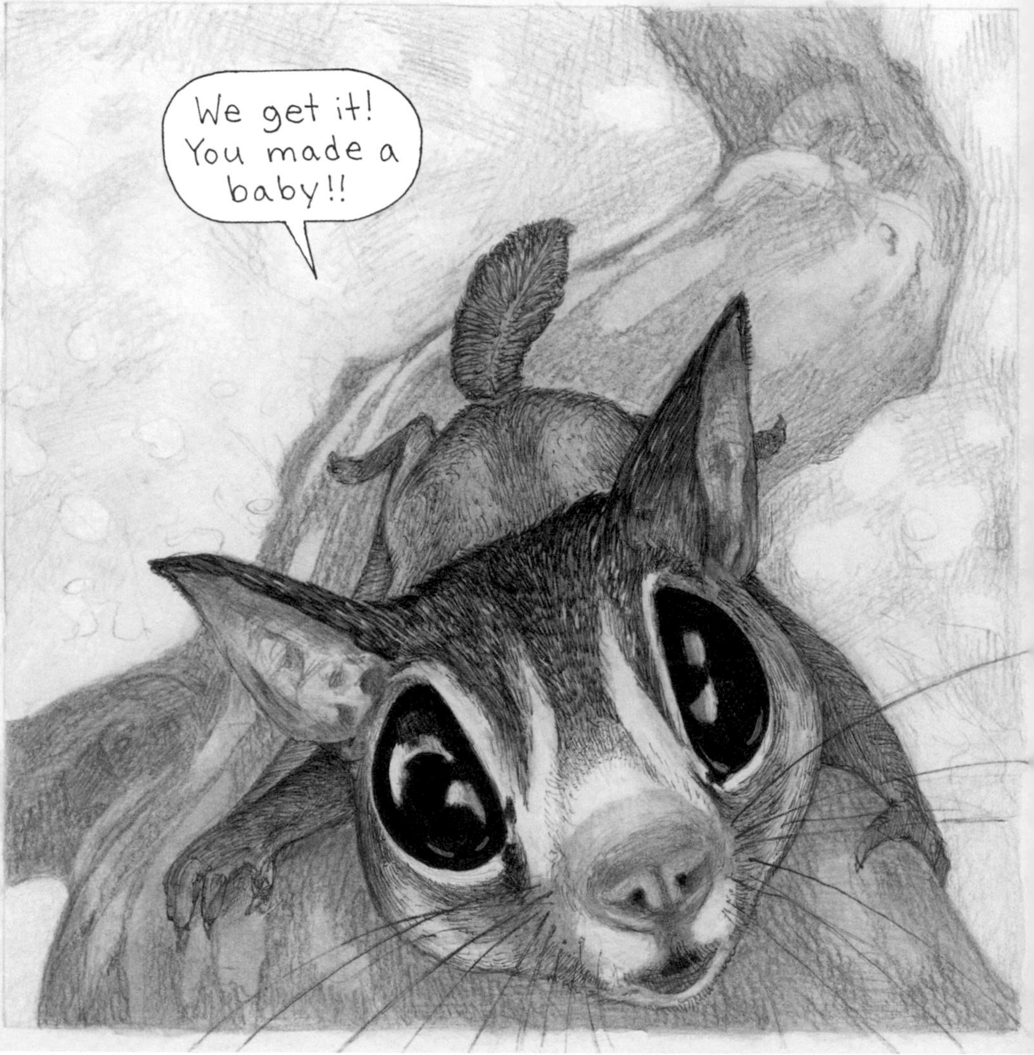
We get it! You made a baby!!

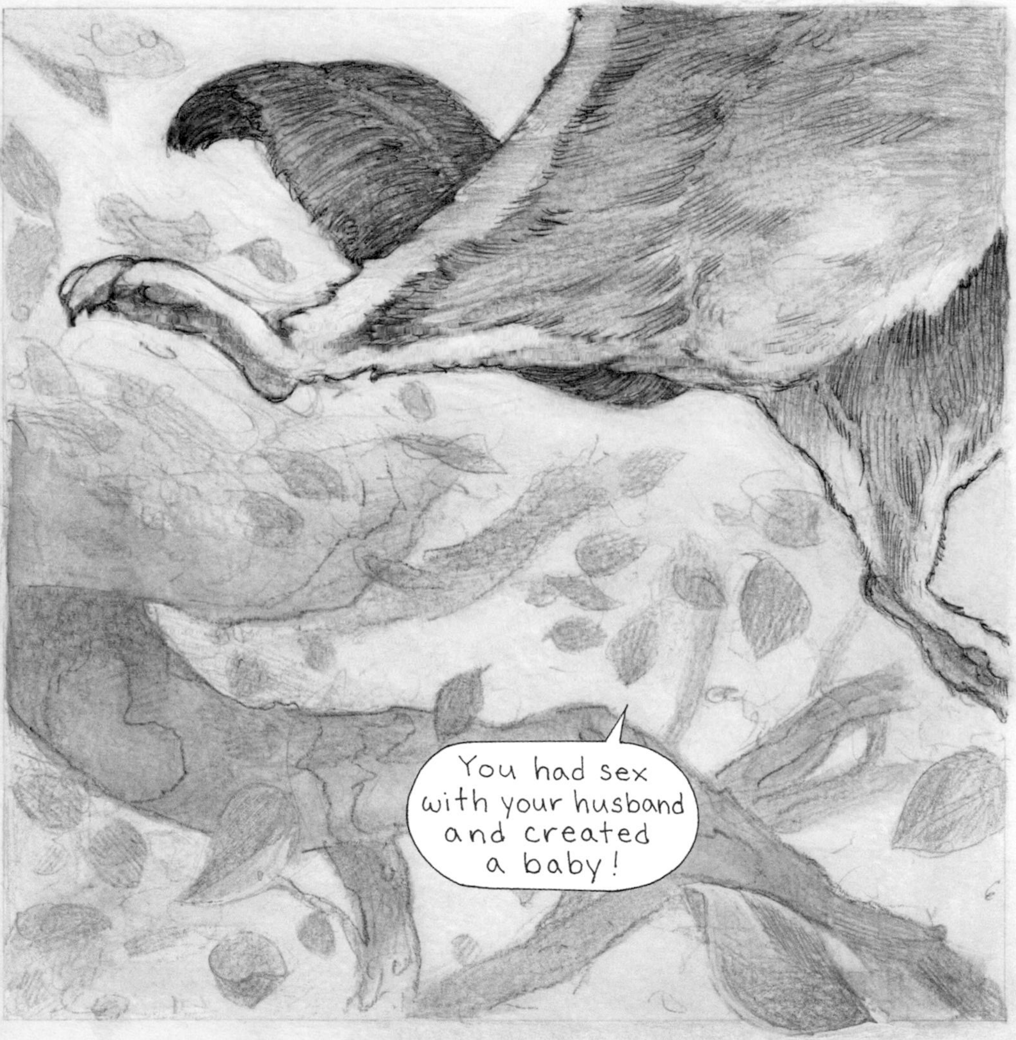
You had sex with your husband and created a baby!

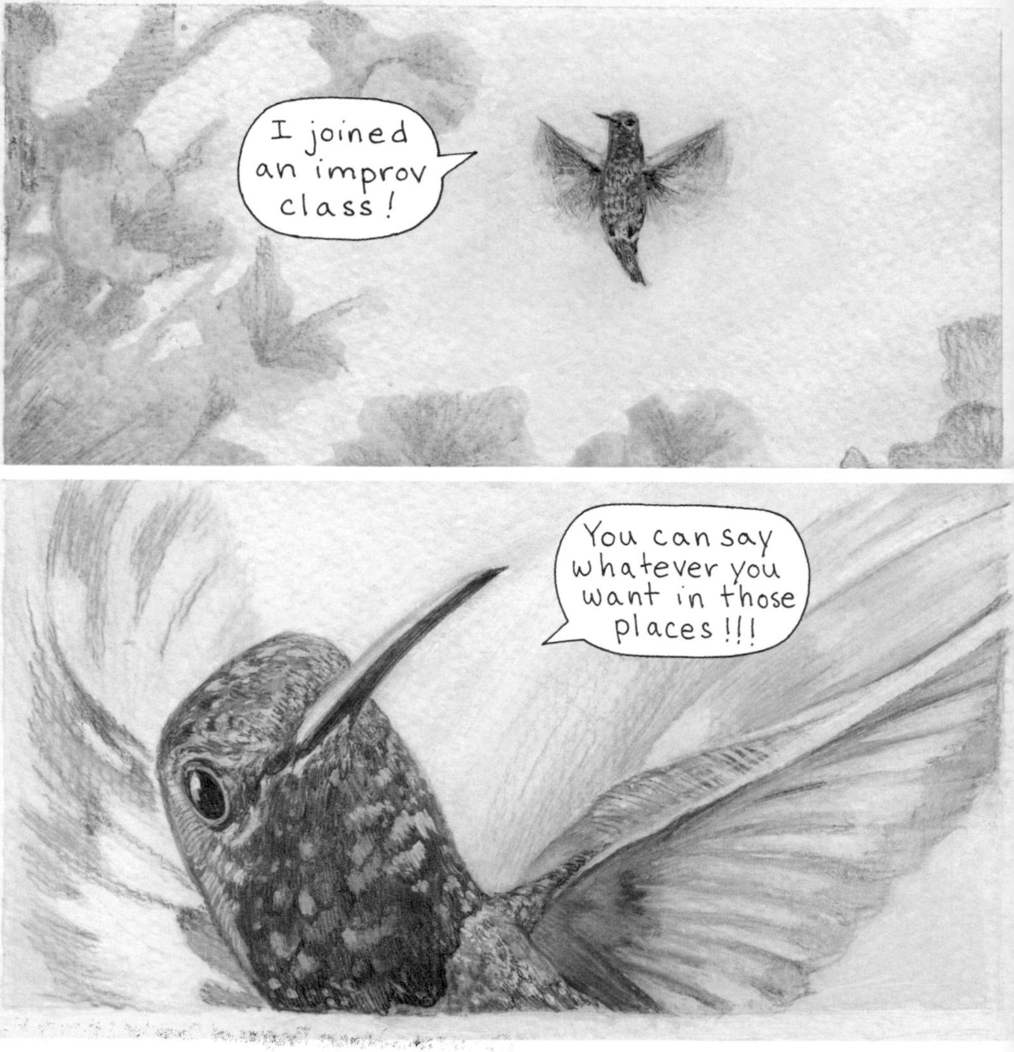
I joined an improv class!
You can say whatever you want in those places!!!

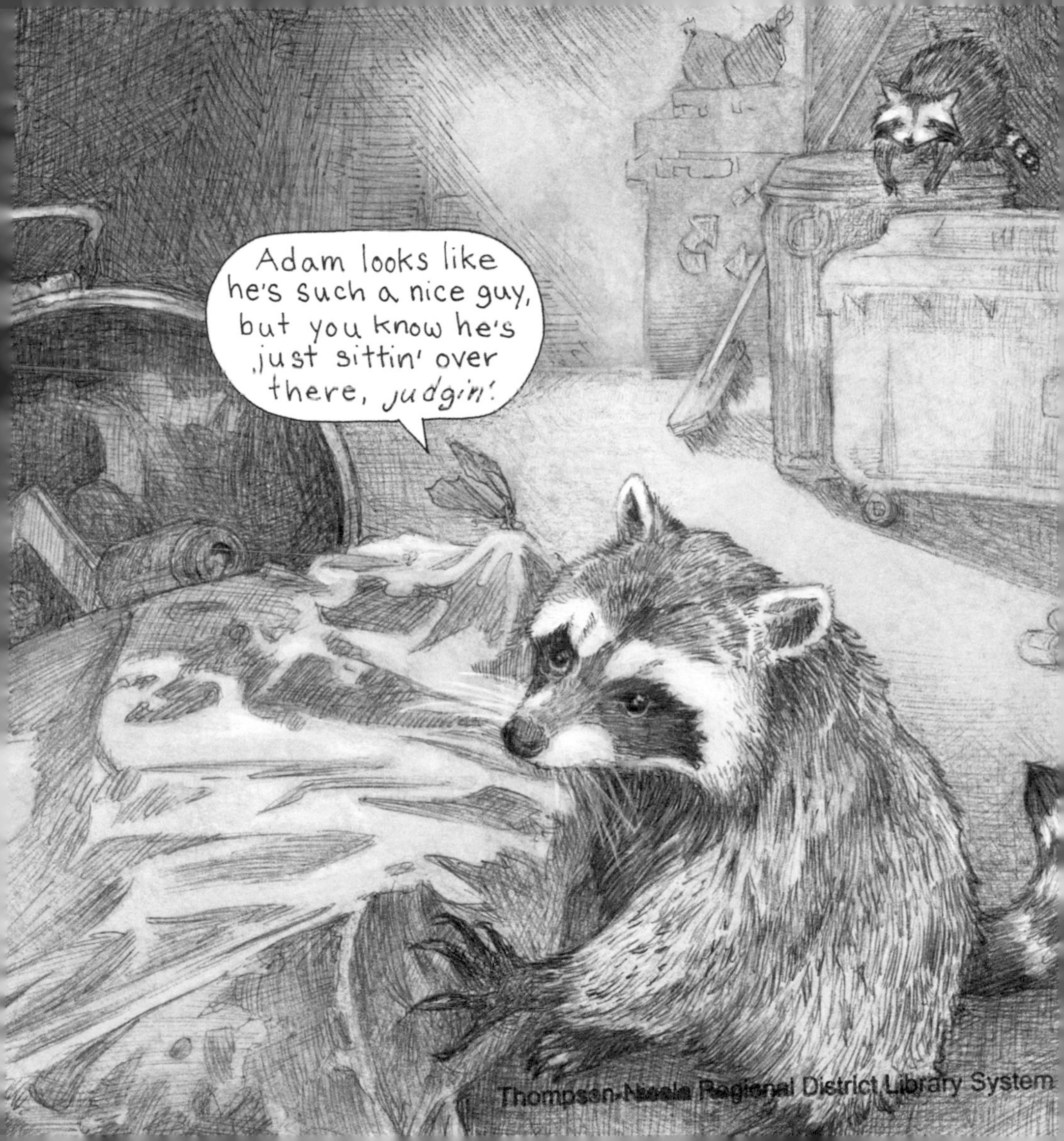
Adam looks like he's such a nice guy, but you know he's just sittin' over there, *judgin'!*

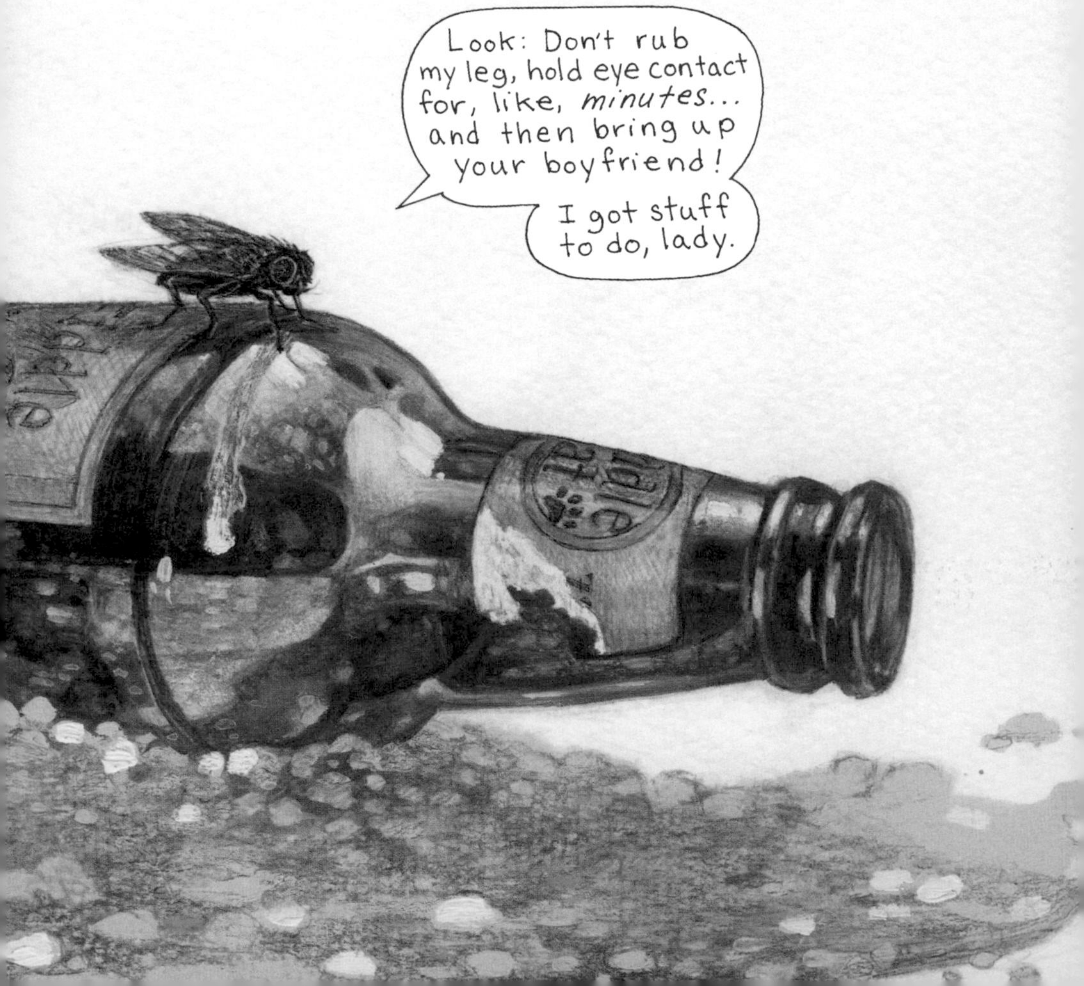
Look: Don't rub my leg, hold eye contact for, like, *minutes*... and then bring up your boyfriend!
I got stuff to do, lady.

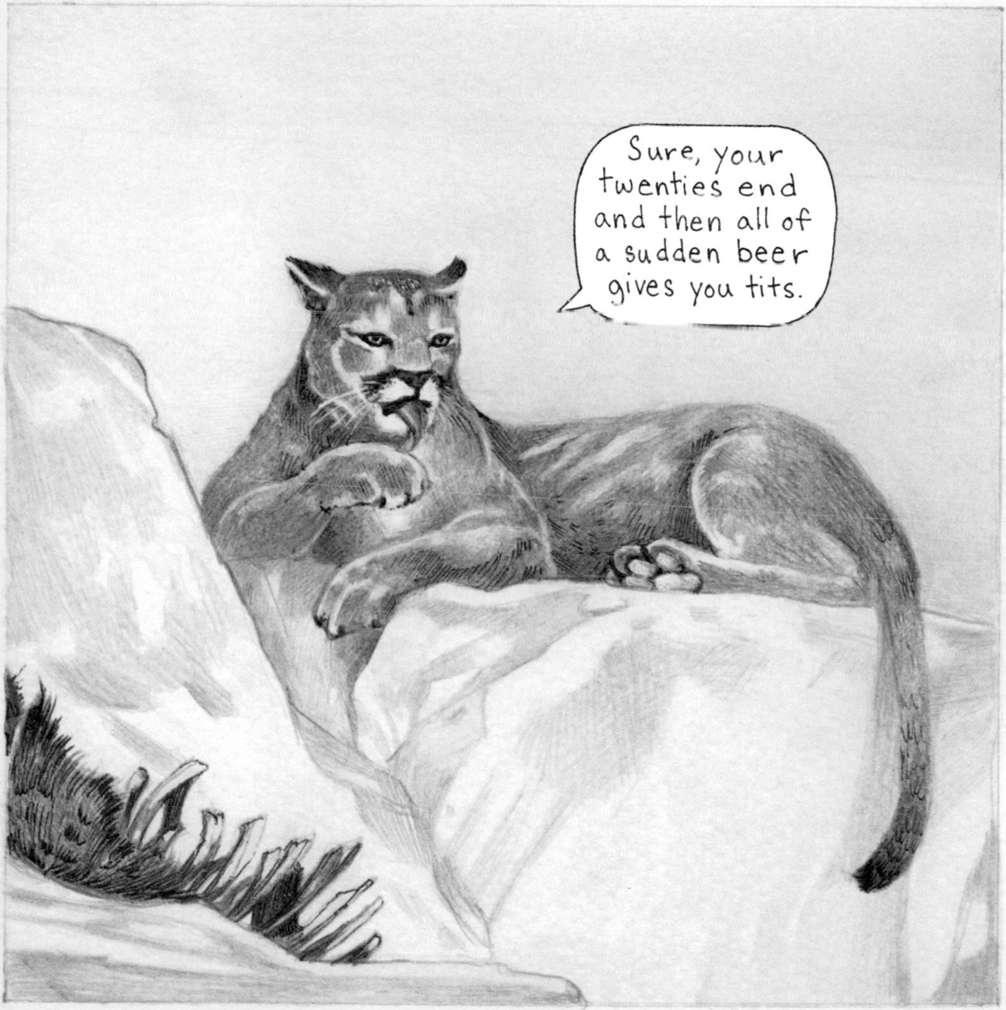
Sure, your twenties end and then all of a sudden beer gives you tits.

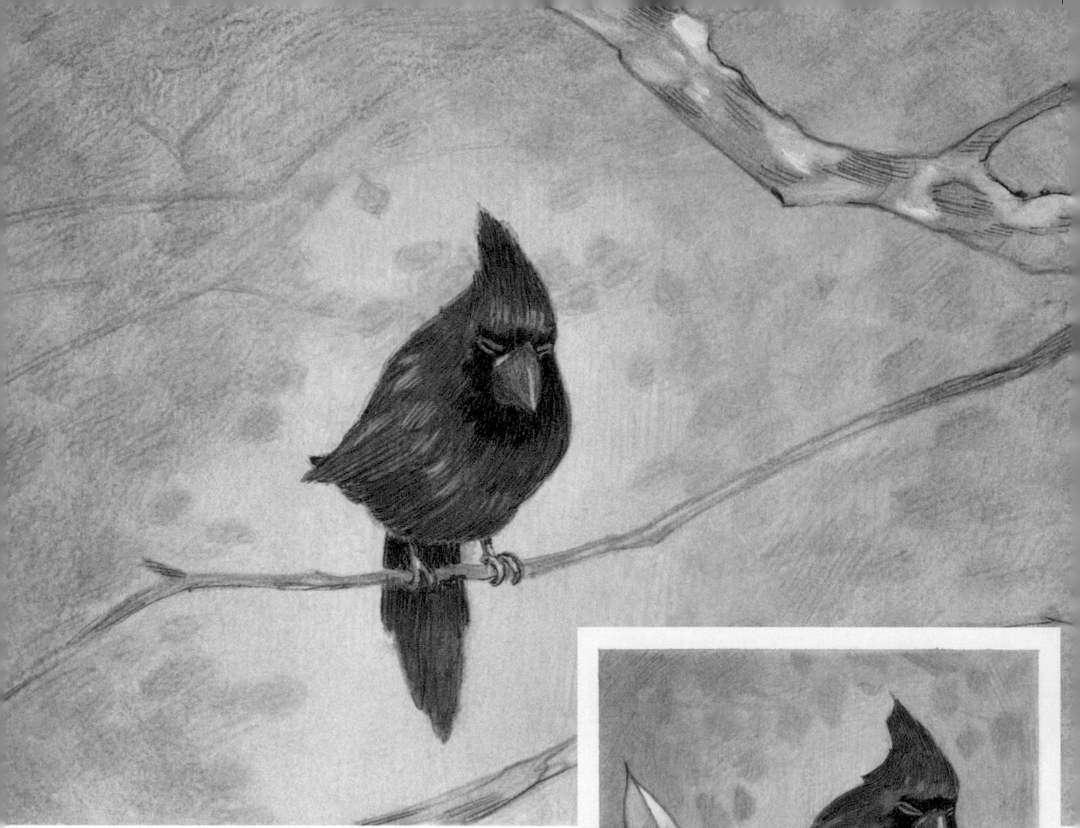

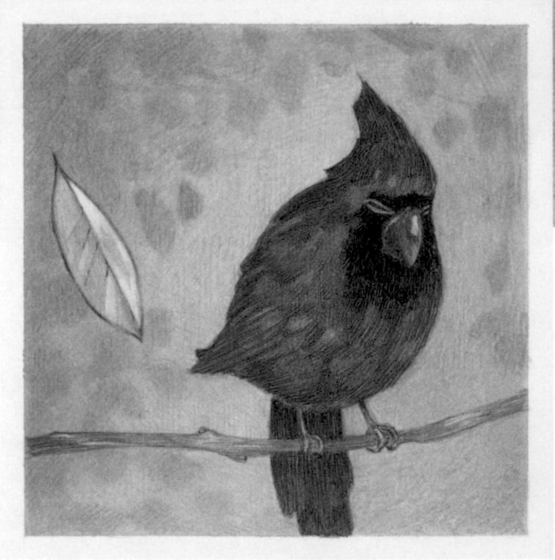

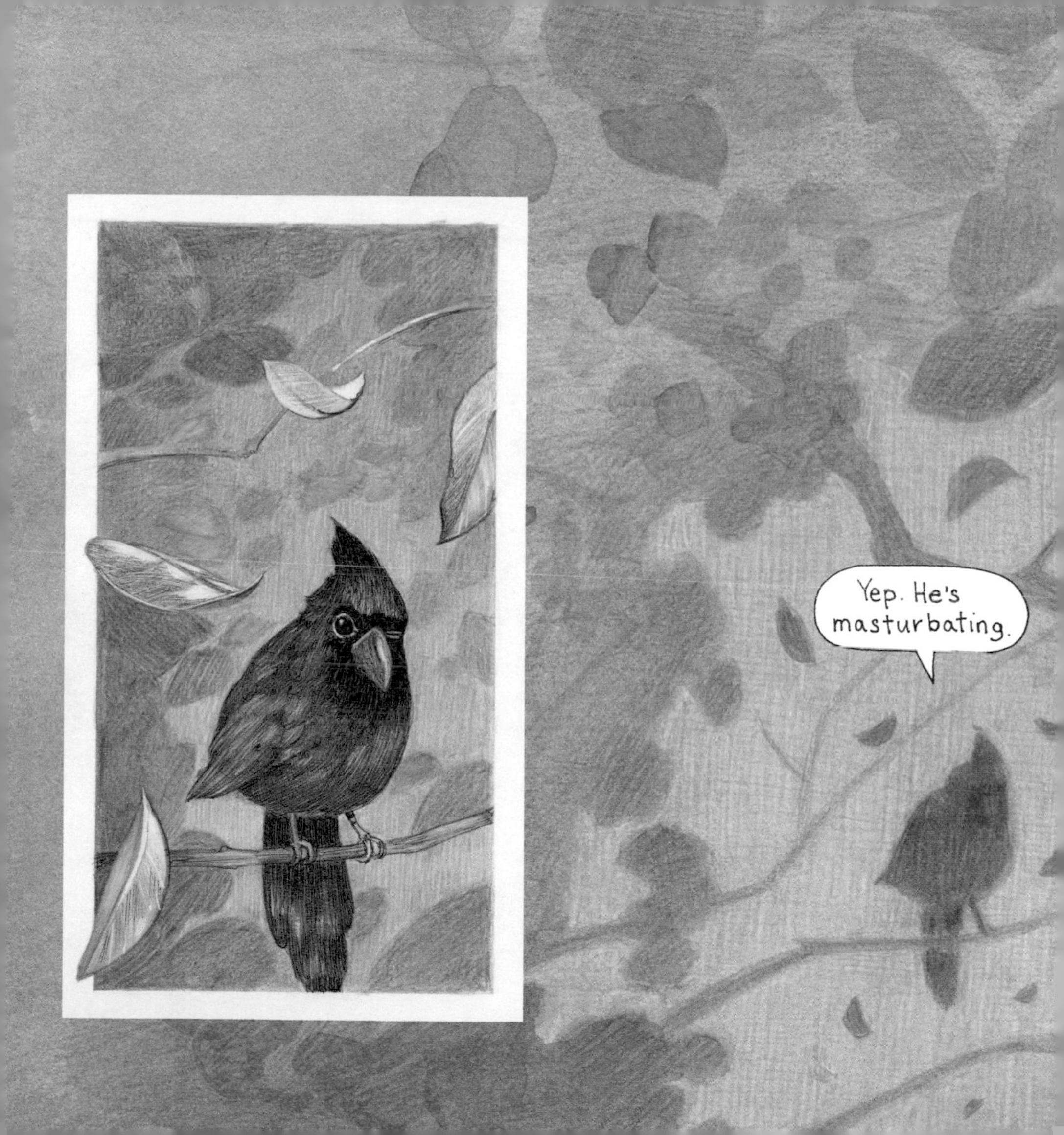
Yep. He's masturbating.

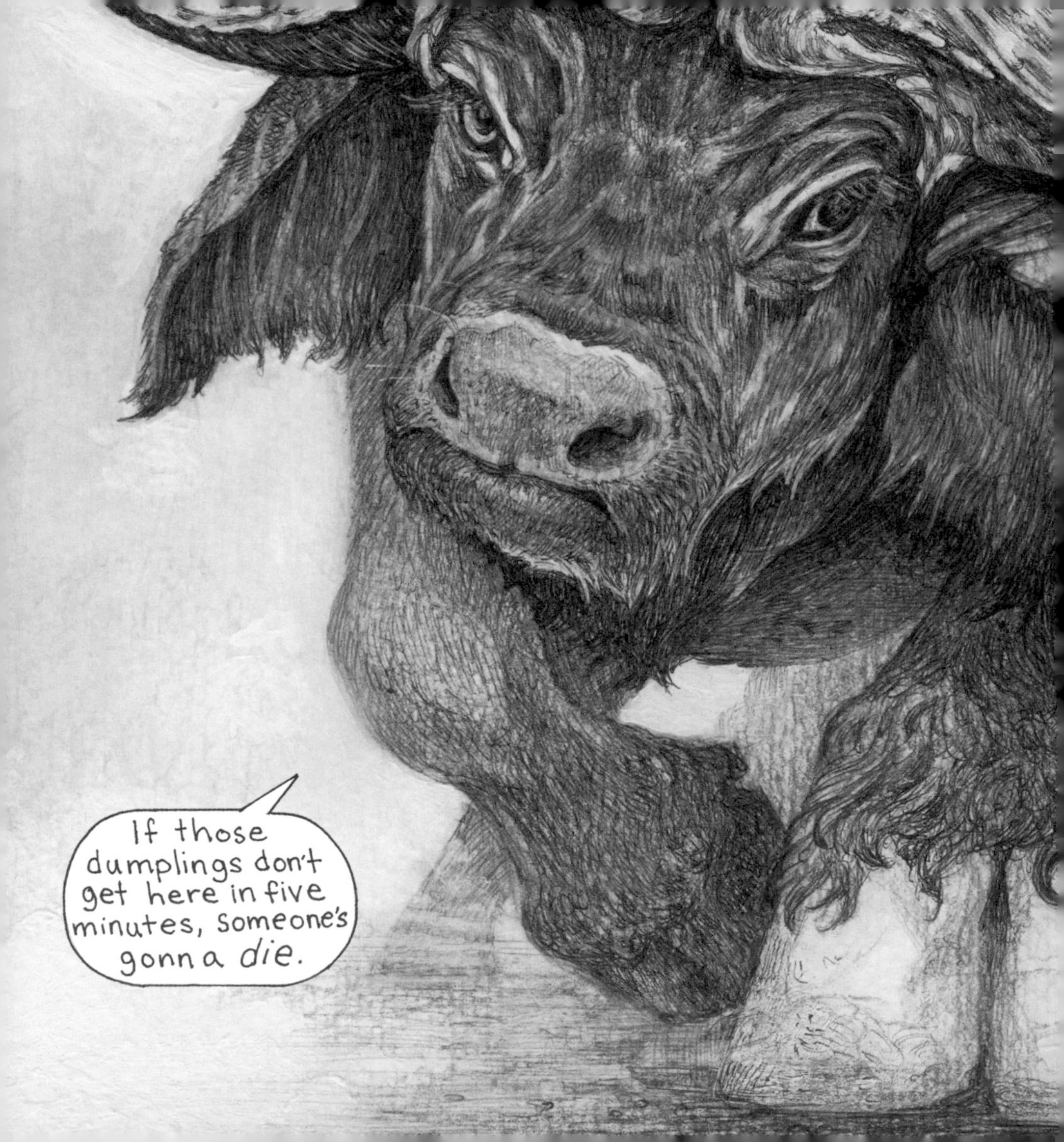
If those dumplings don't get here in five minutes, someone's gonna *die*.

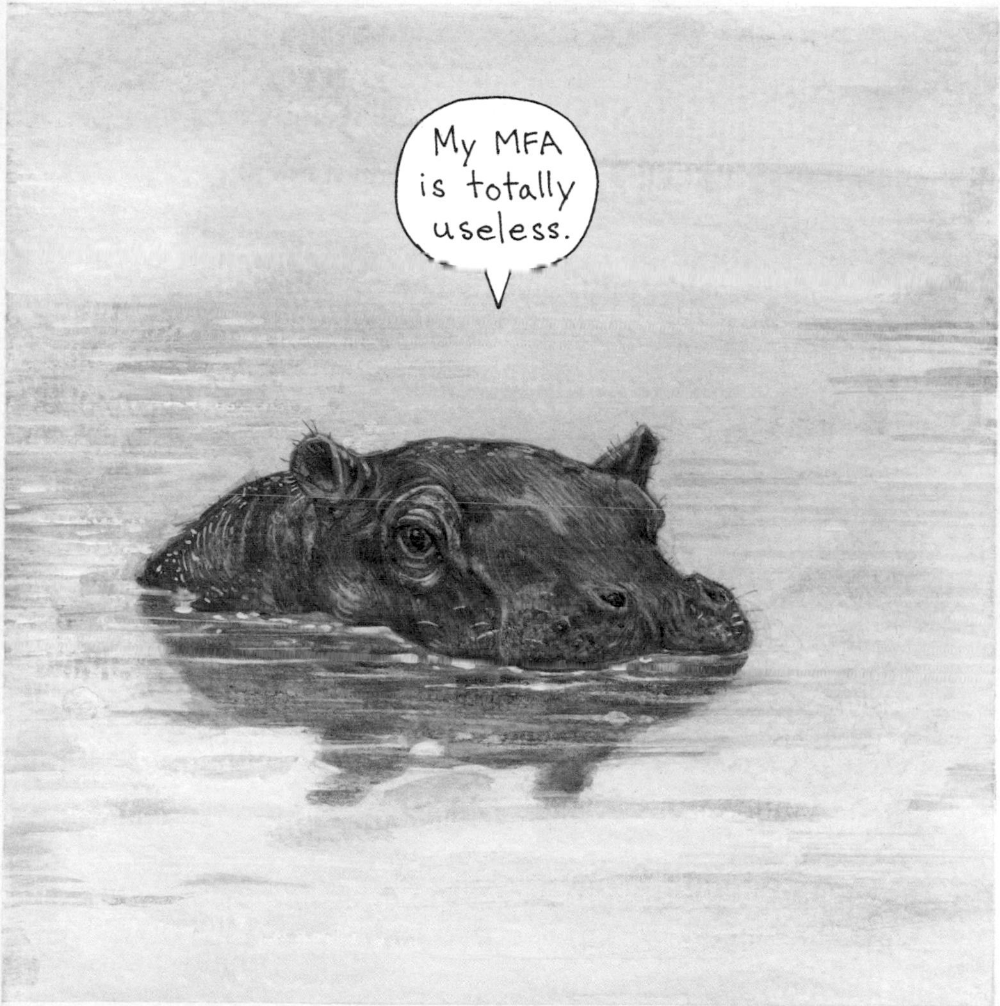
My MFA is totally useless.

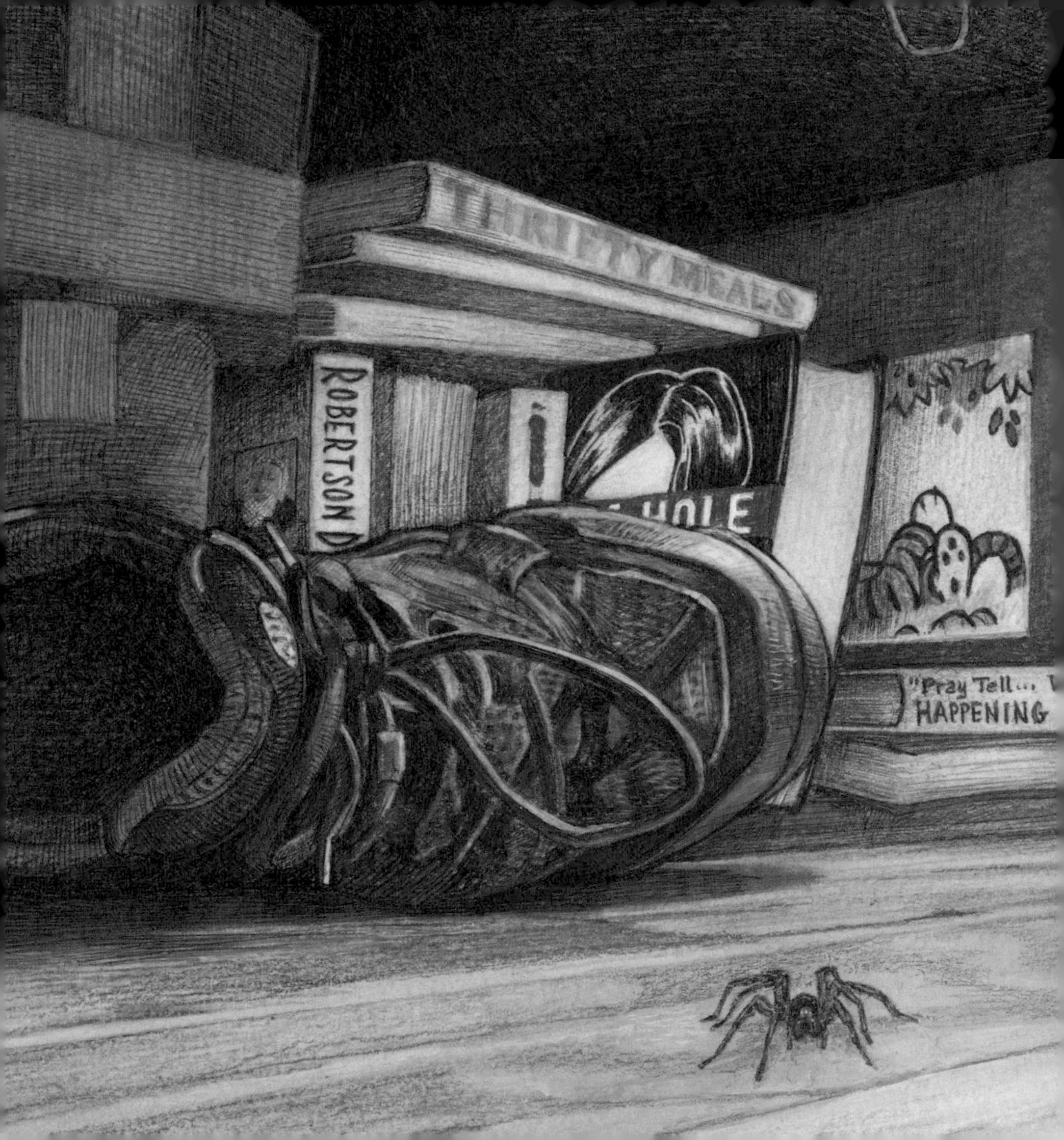
THRIFTY MEALS
ROBERTSON D
HOLE
"Pray Tell...
HAPPENING

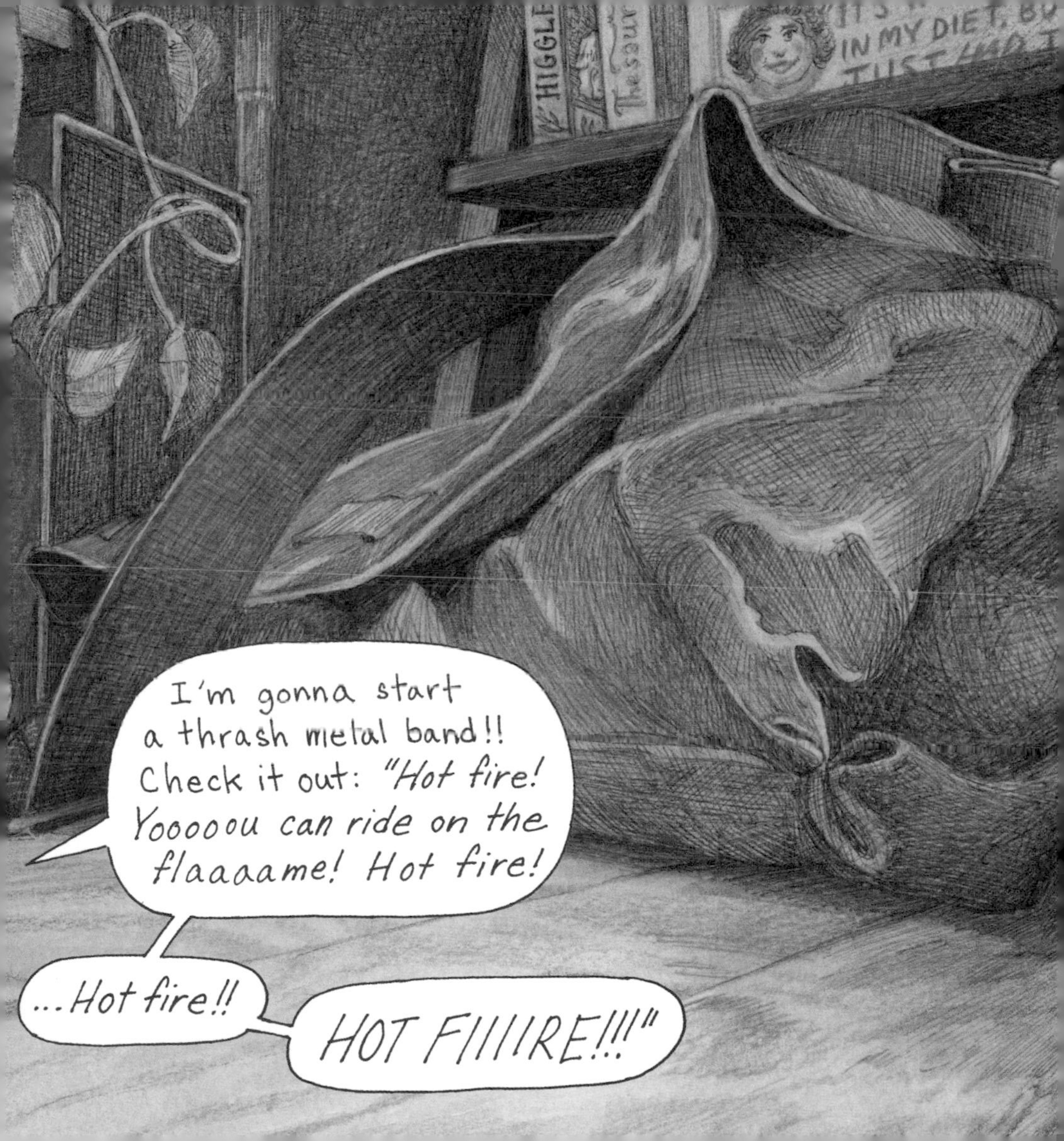
I'm gonna start a thrash metal band!! Check it out: "Hot fire! Yooooou can ride on the flaaaame! Hot fire!
...Hot fire!!
HOT FIIIIRE!!!"

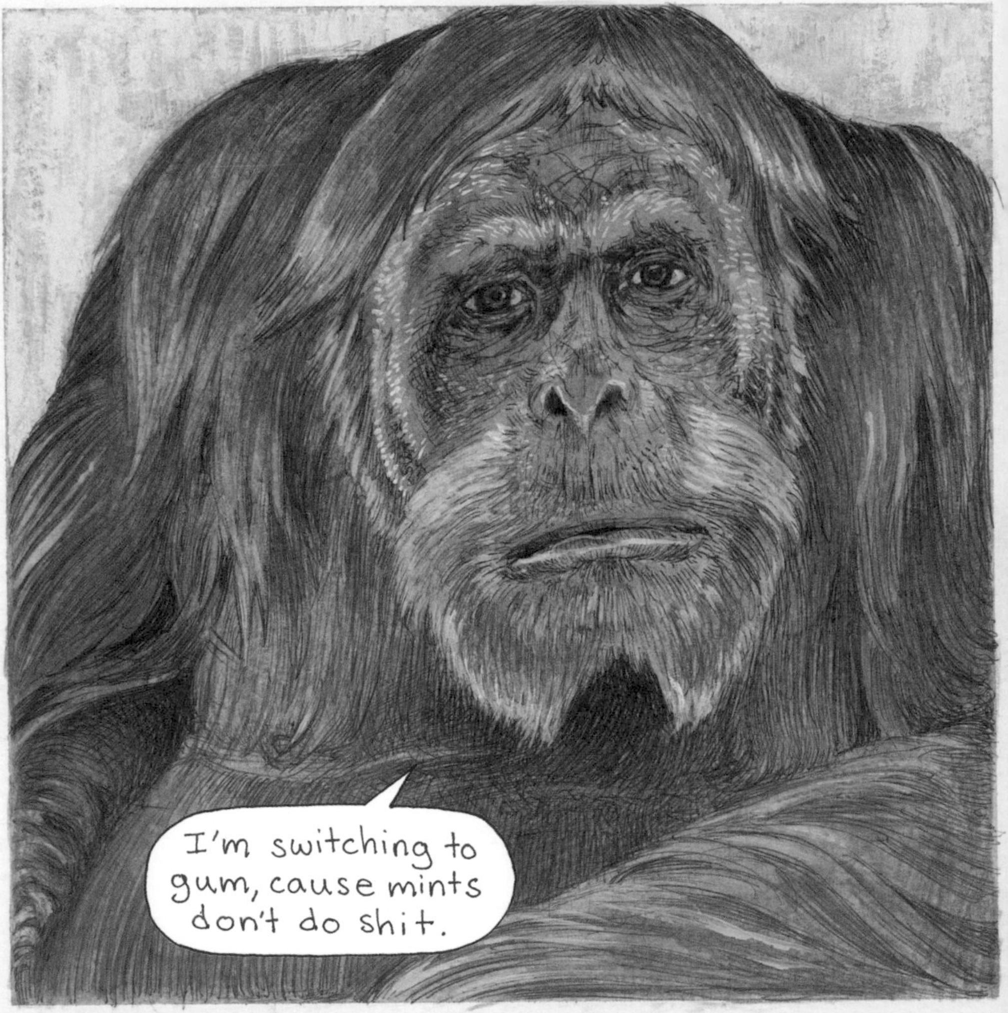
I'm switching to gum, cause mints don't do shit.

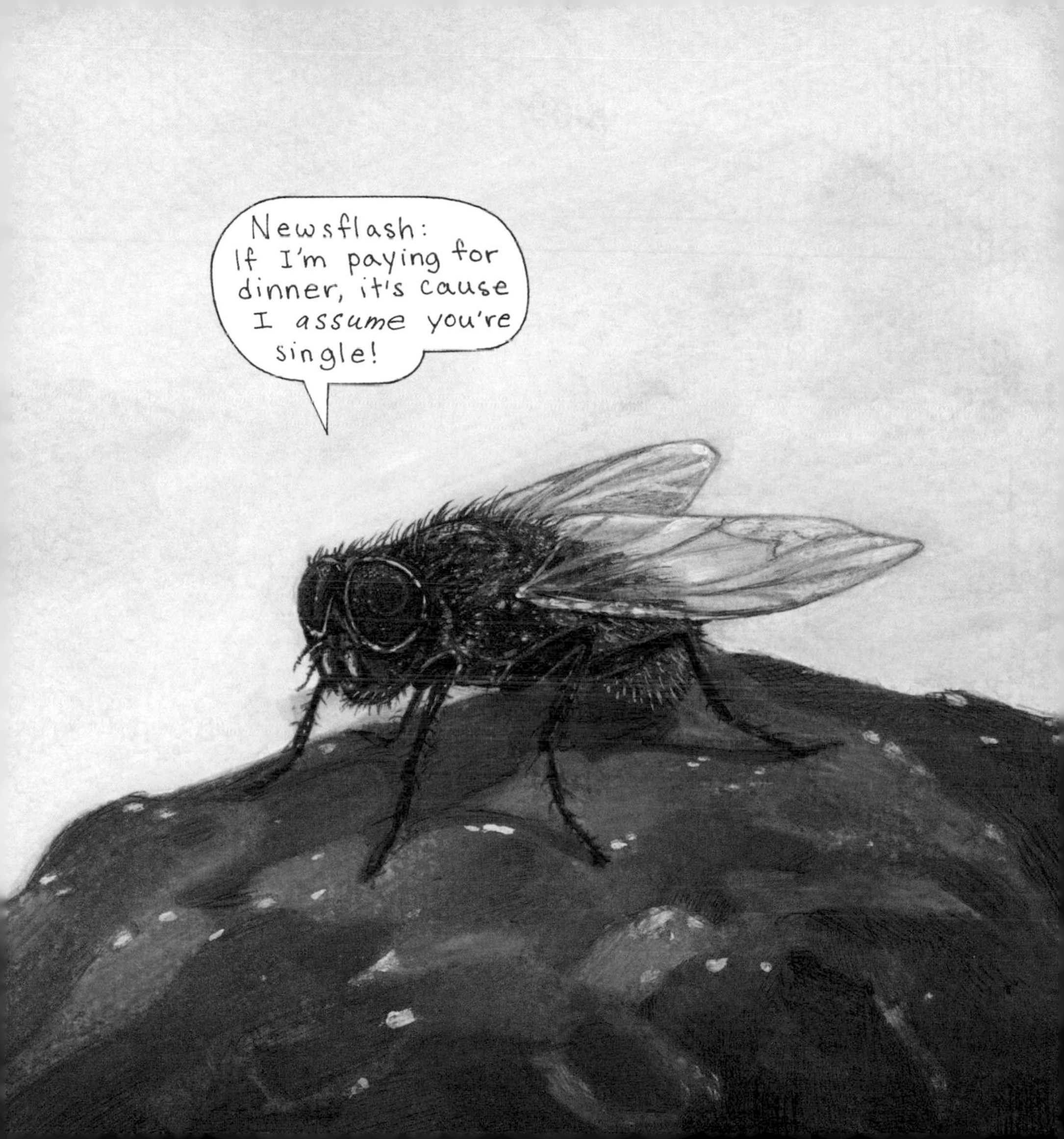
Newsflash: If I'm paying for dinner, it's cause I *assume* you're single!

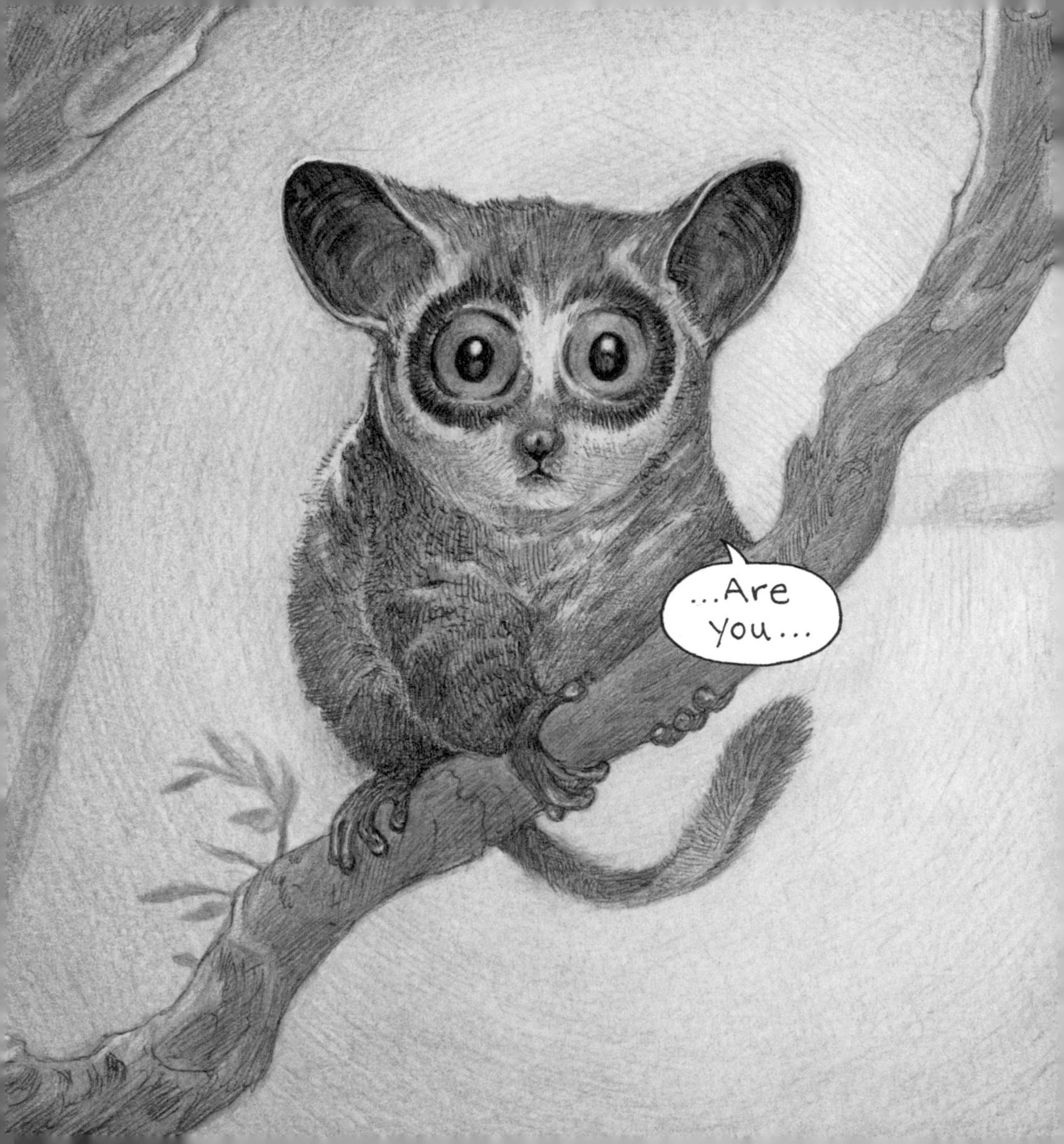
...Are you...

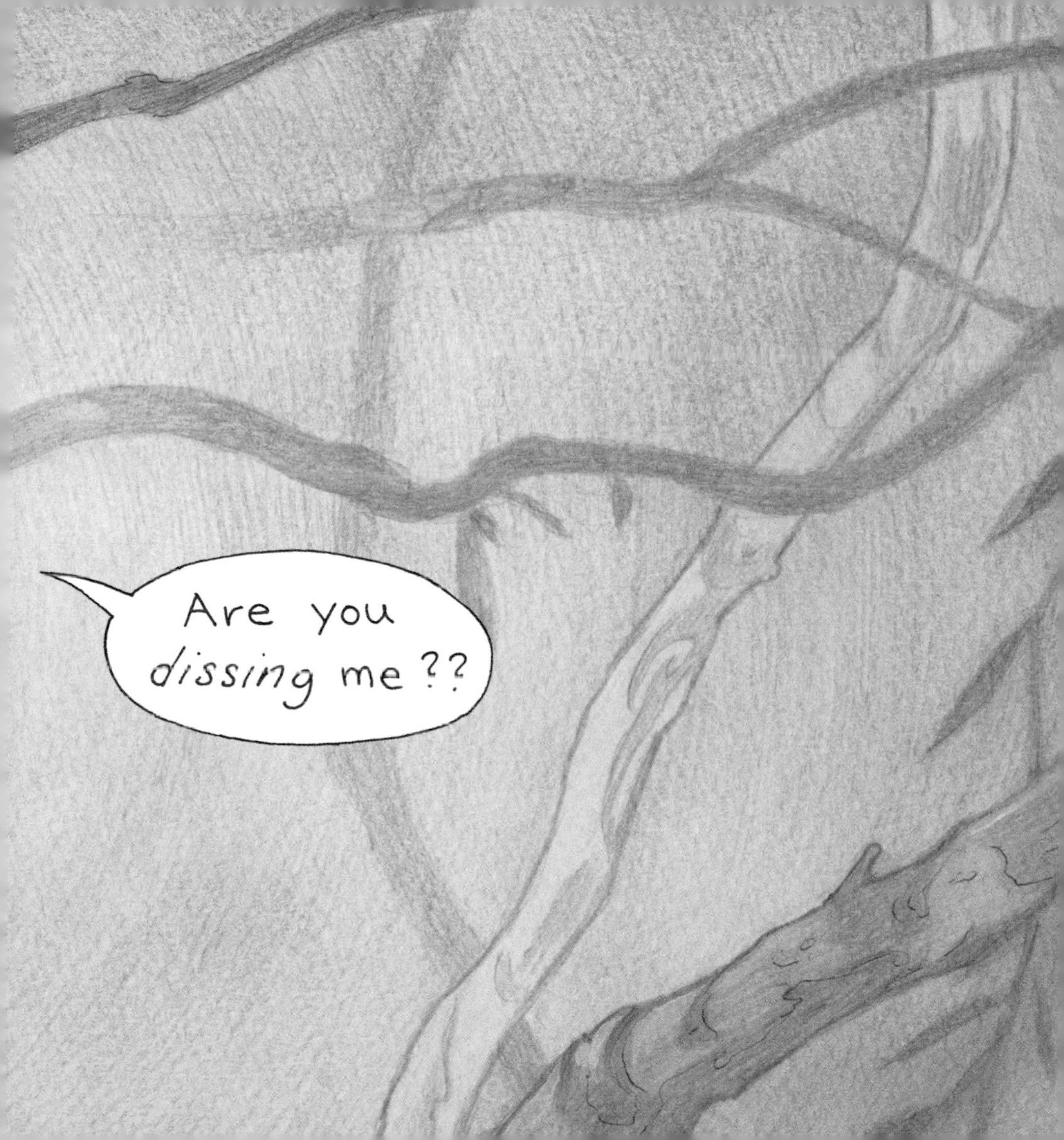
Are you dissing me??

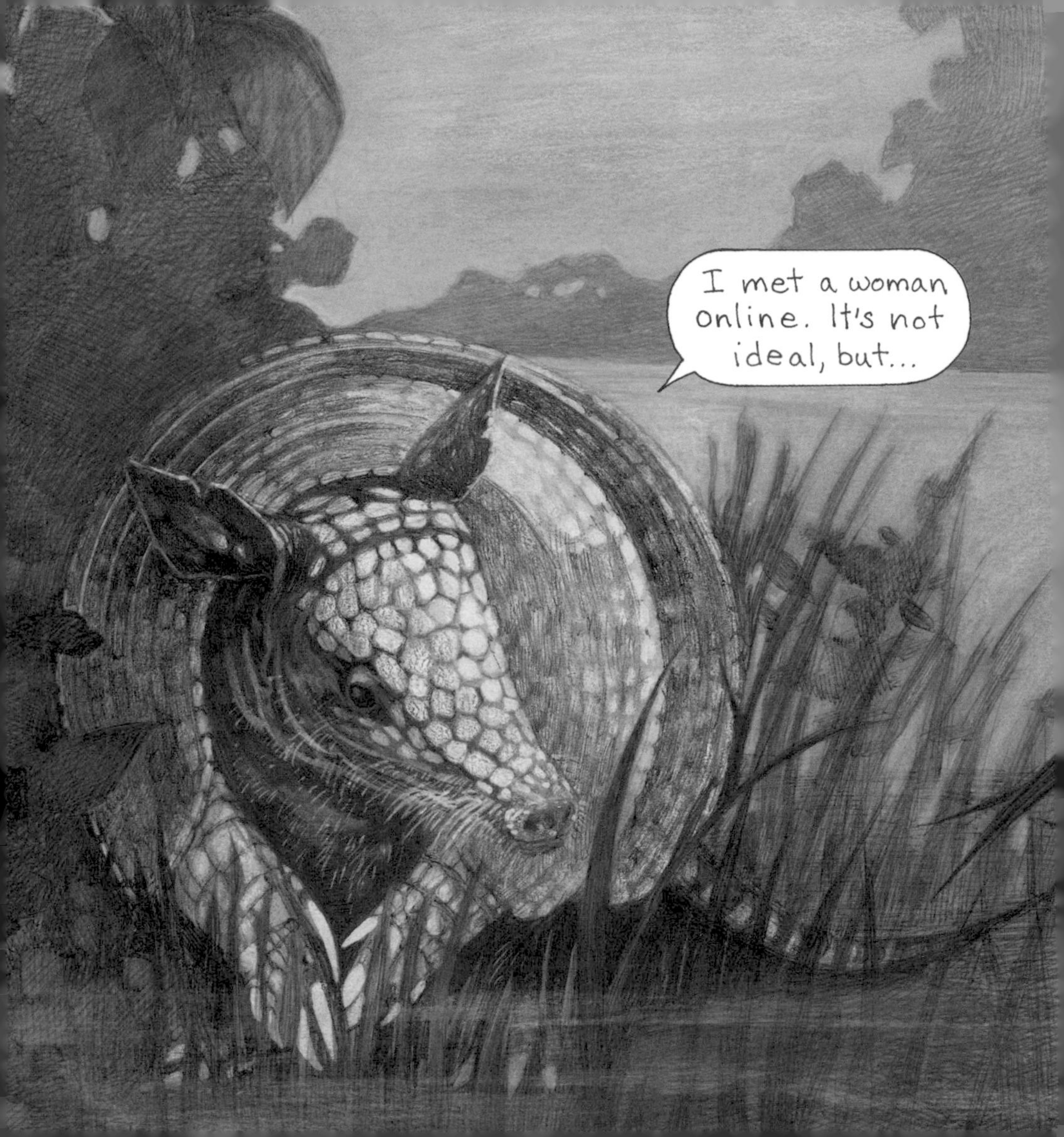
I met a woman online. It's not ideal, but...

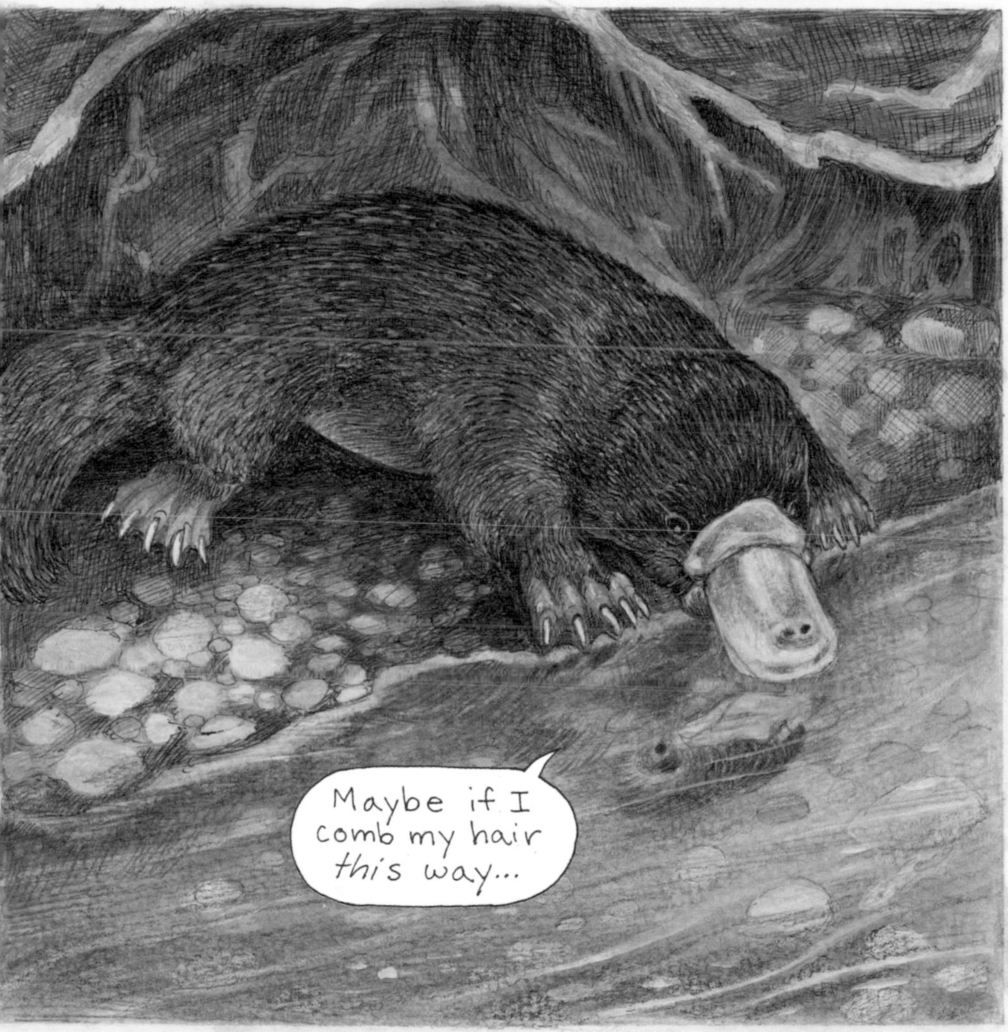
Maybe if I comb my hair this way...

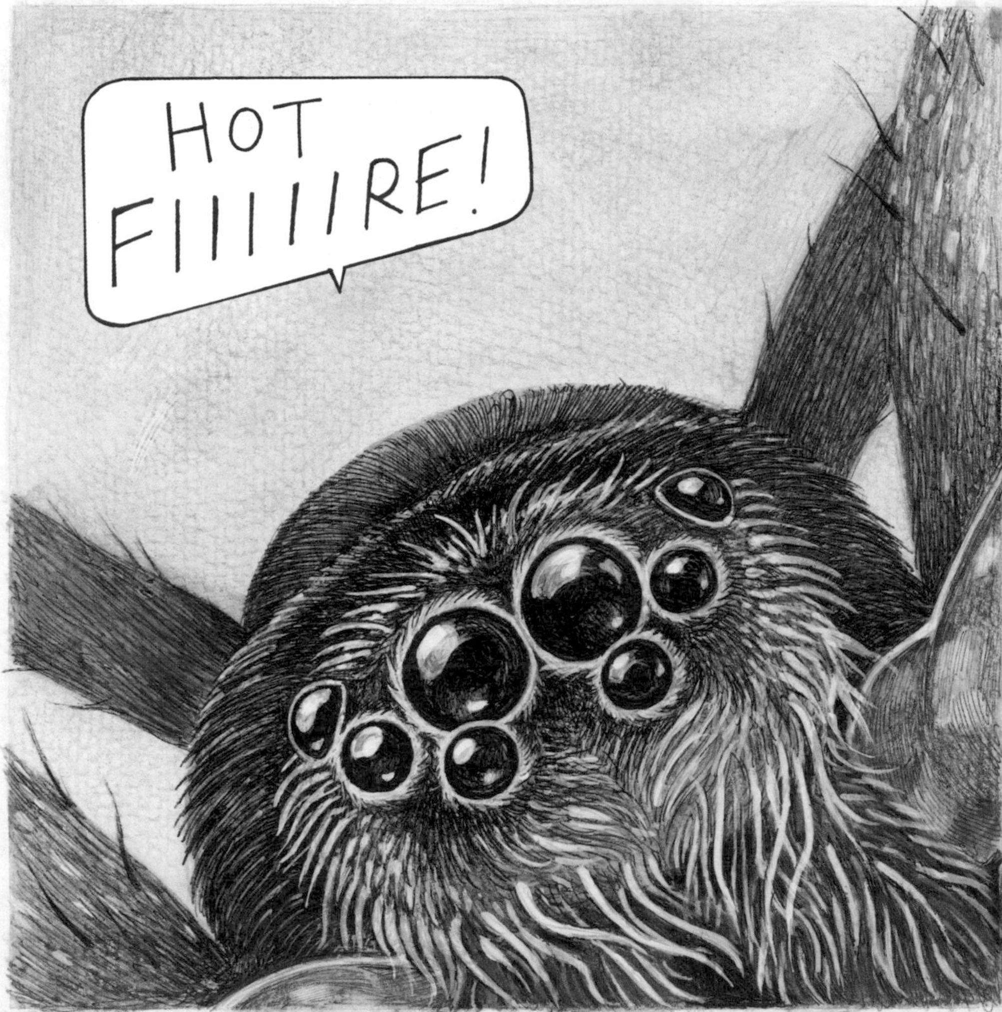
HOT FIIIIRE!

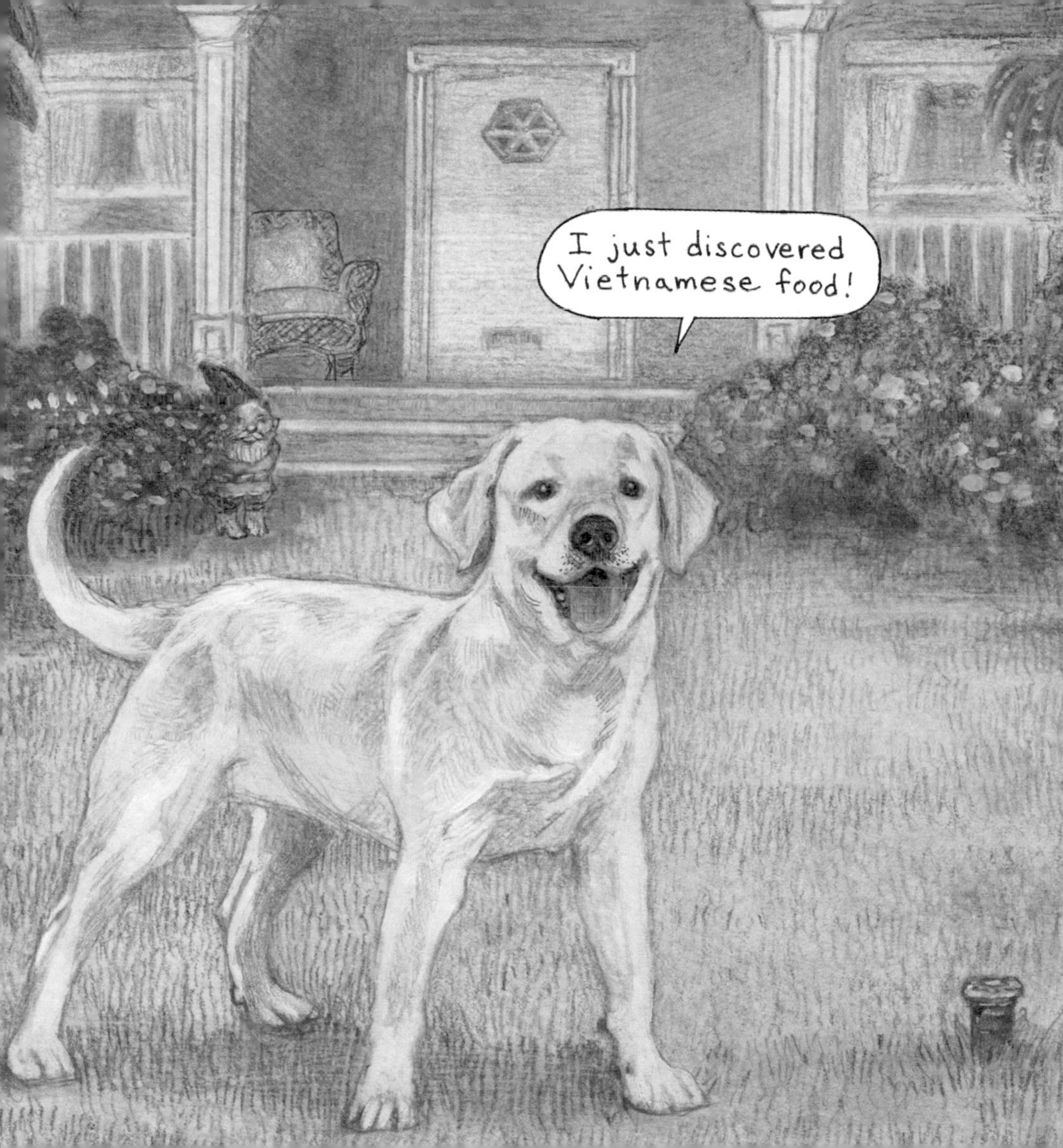
I just discovered Vietnamese food!

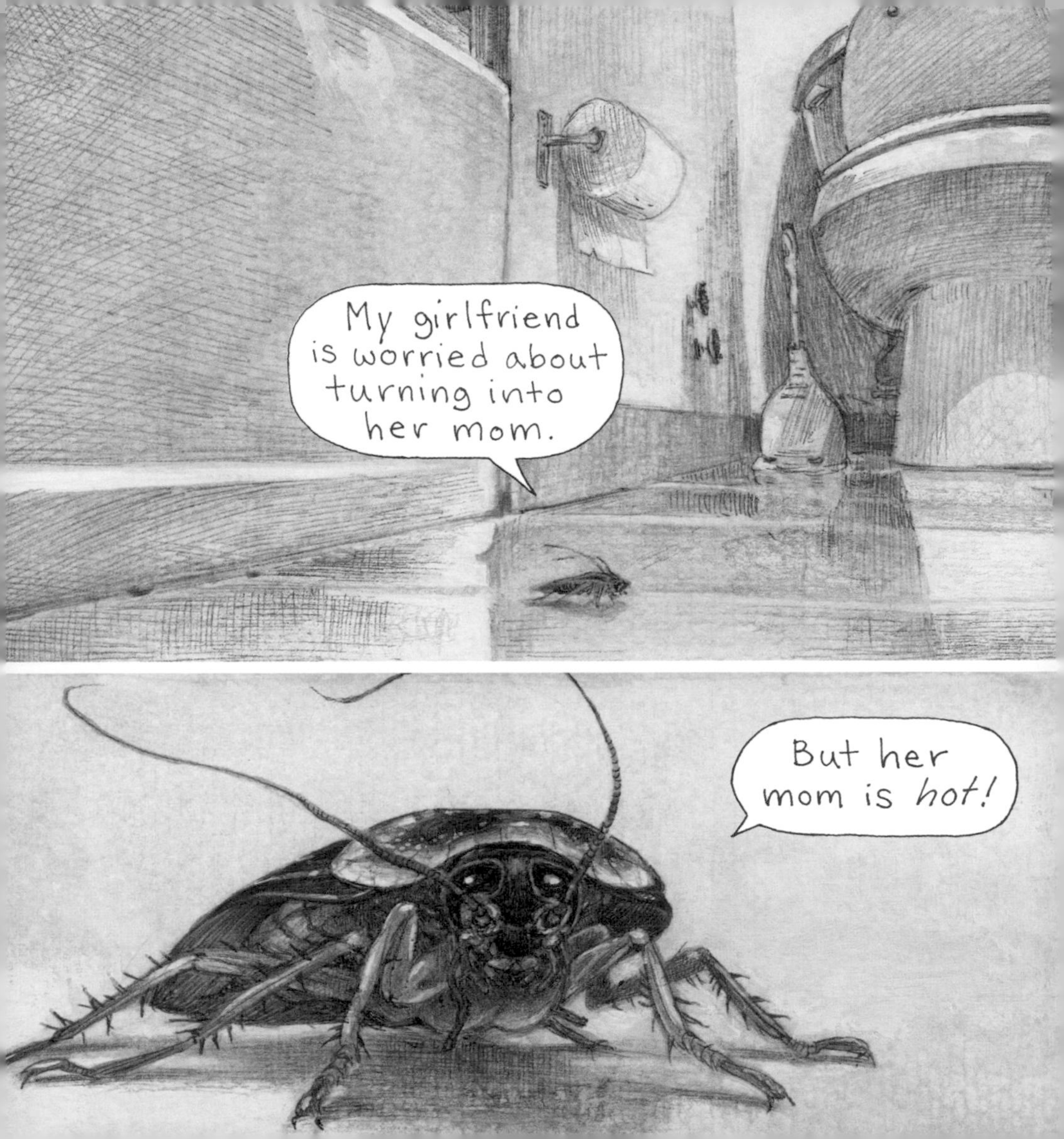
My girlfriend is worried about turning into her mom.
But her mom is *hot!*

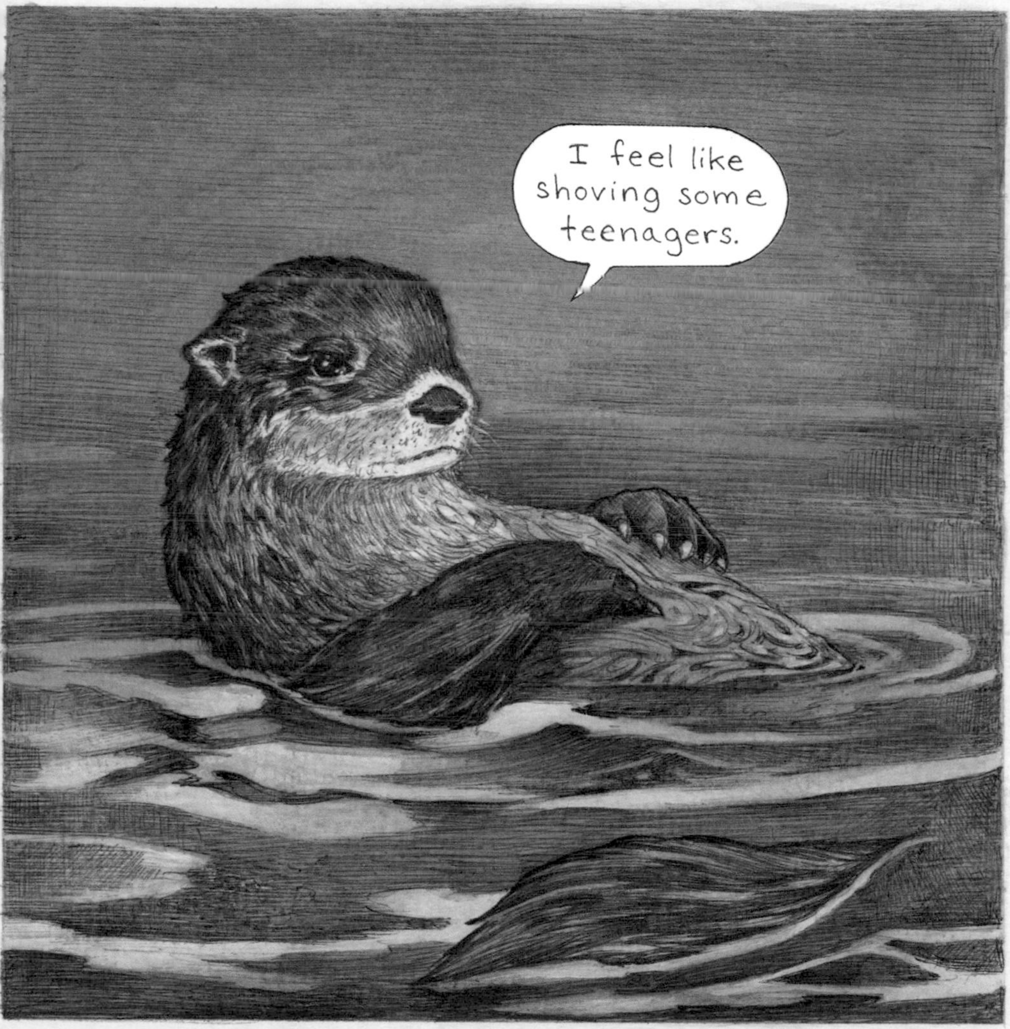
I feel like shoving some teenagers.

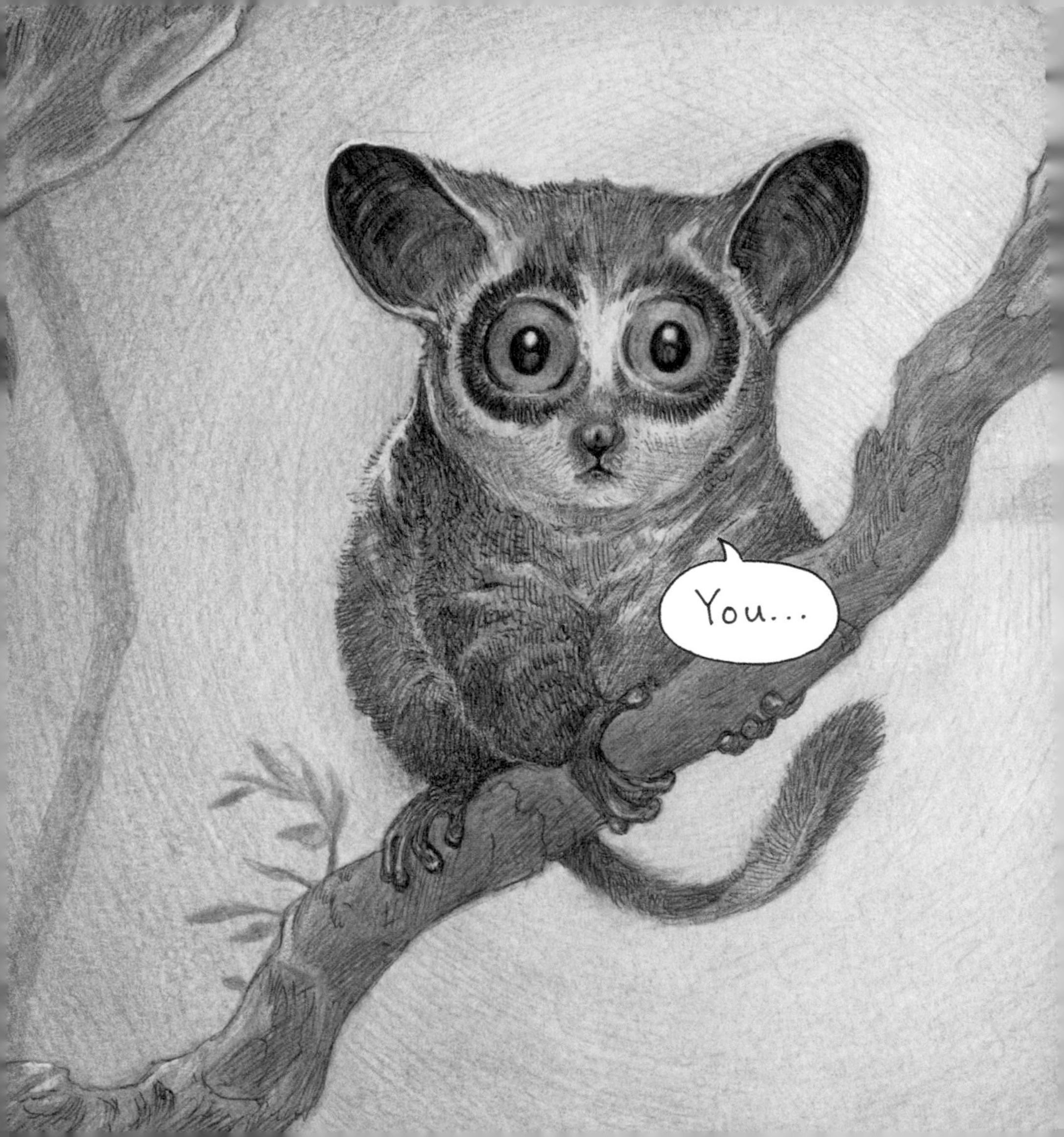
You...

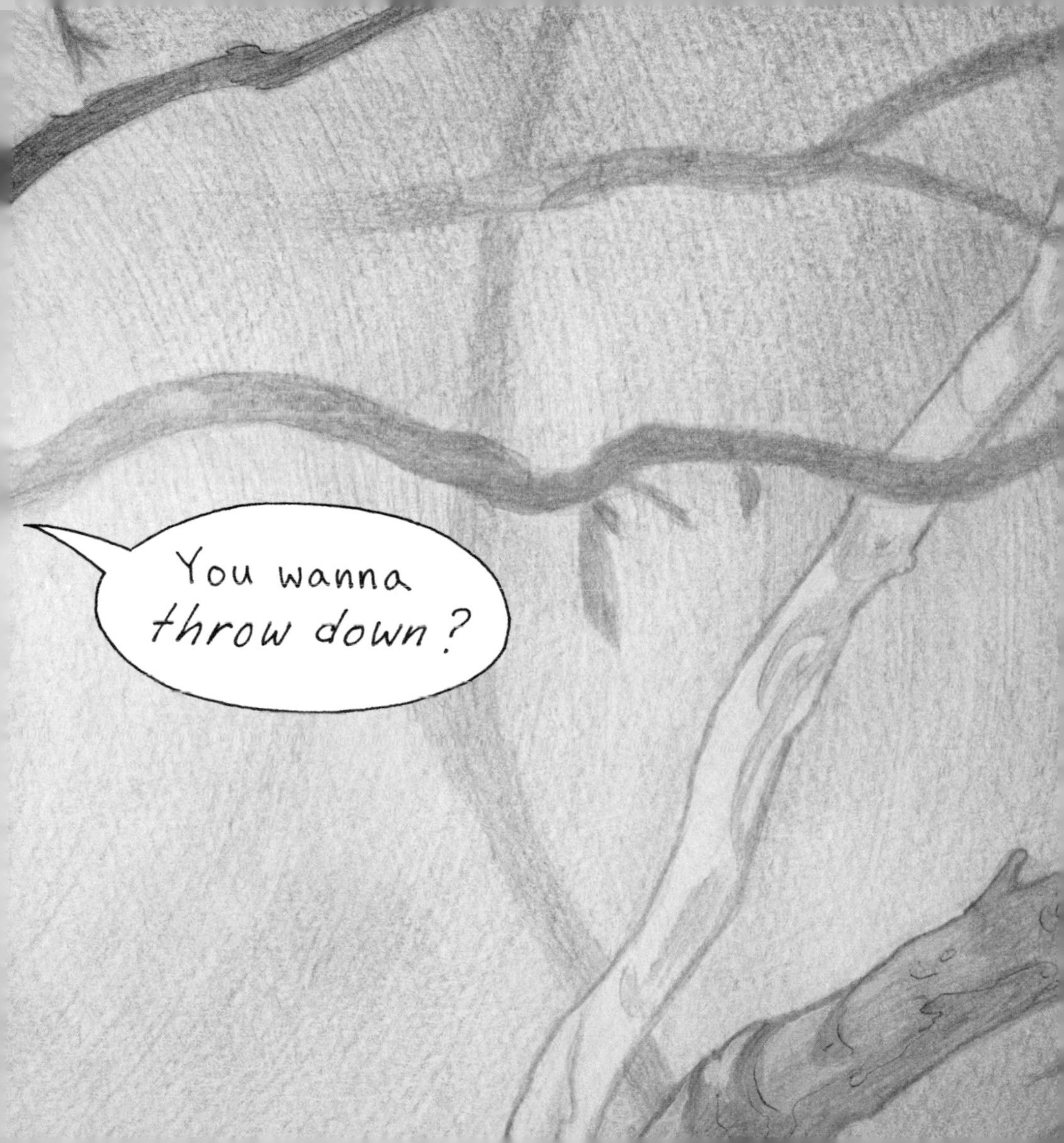
You wanna throw down?

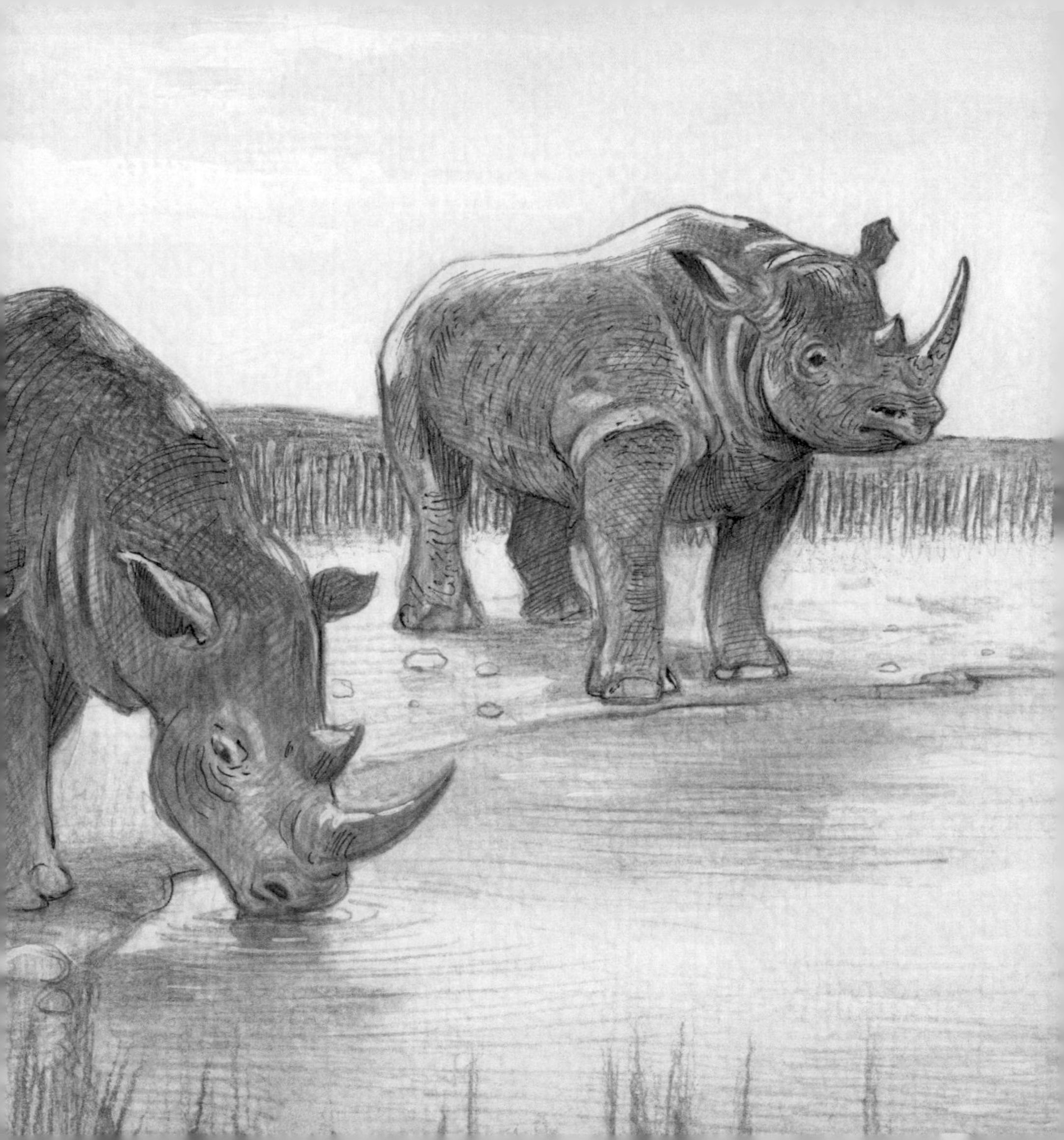

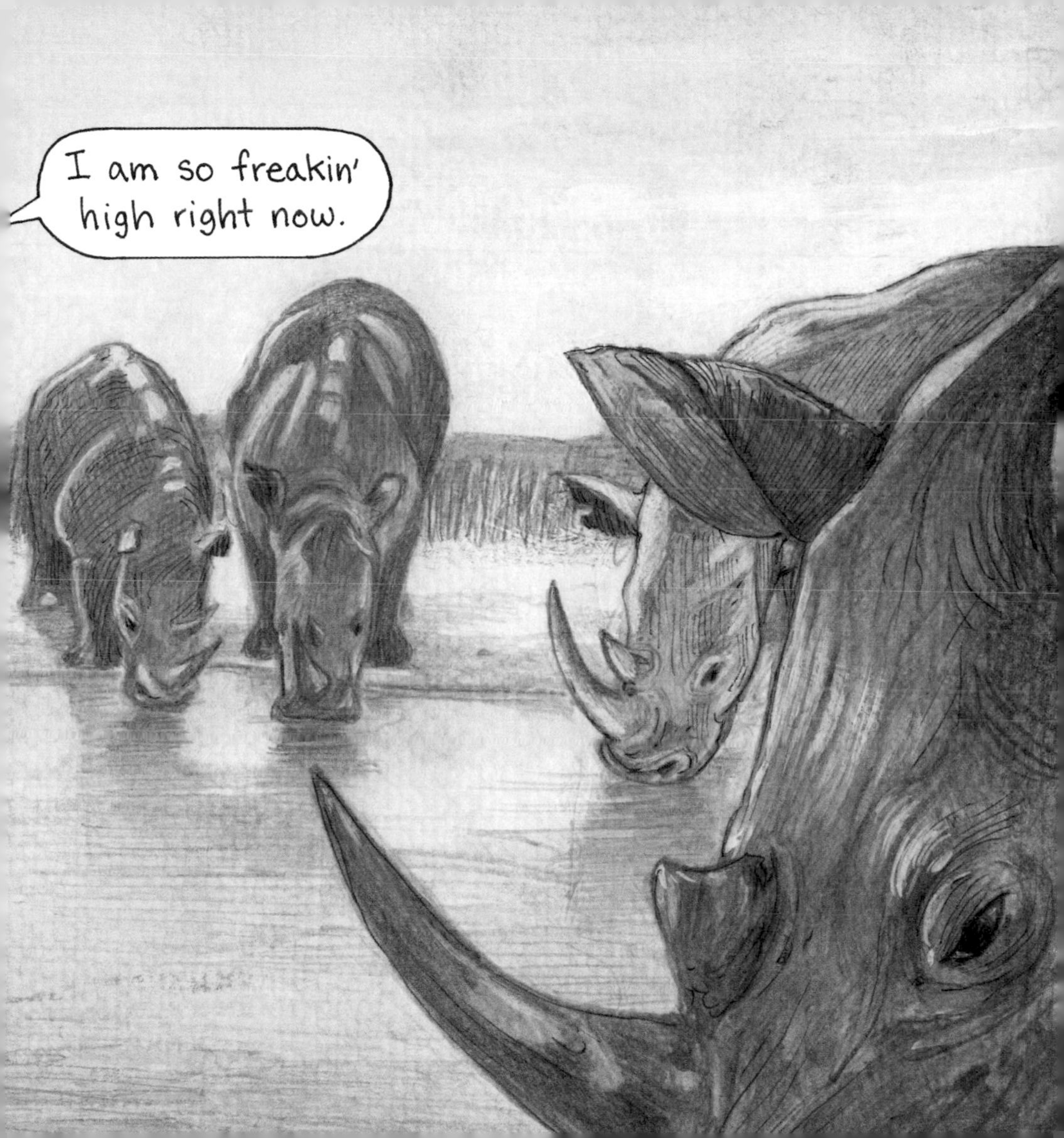
I am so freakin' high right now.

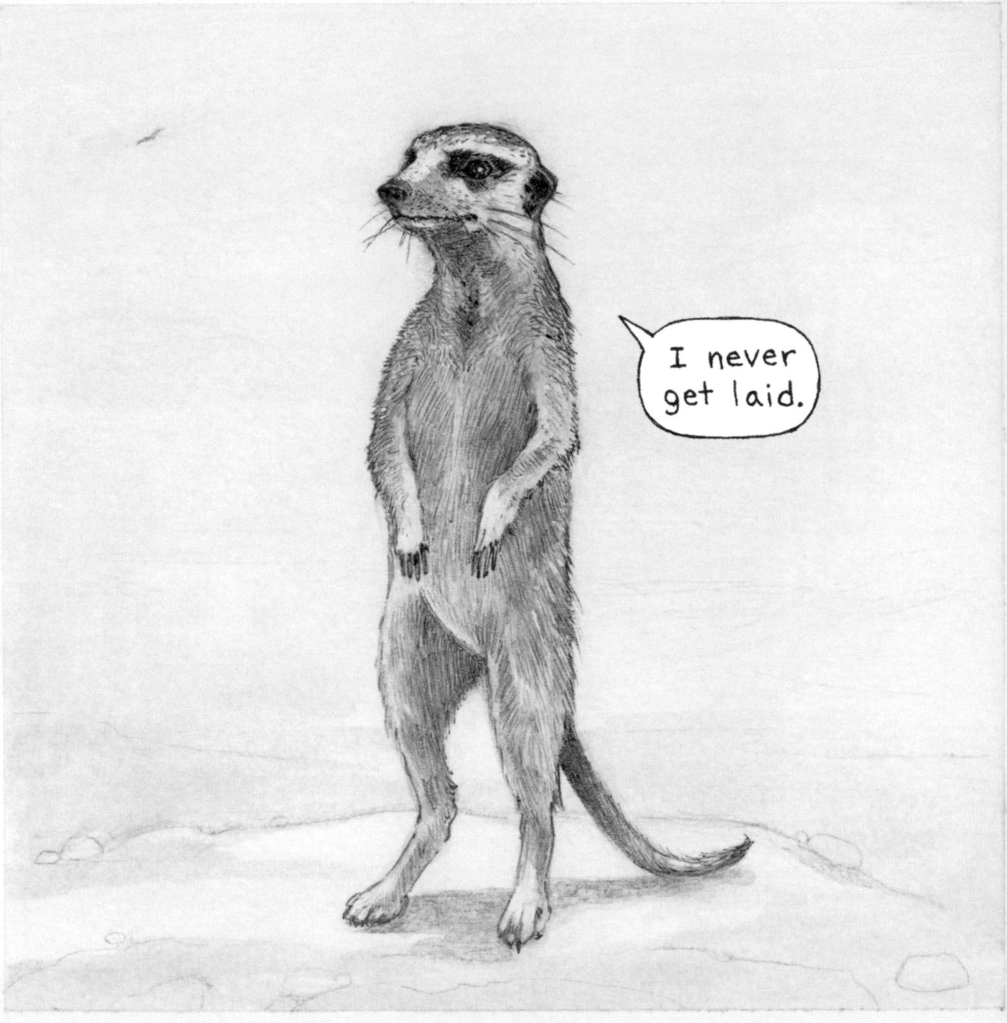
I never get laid.

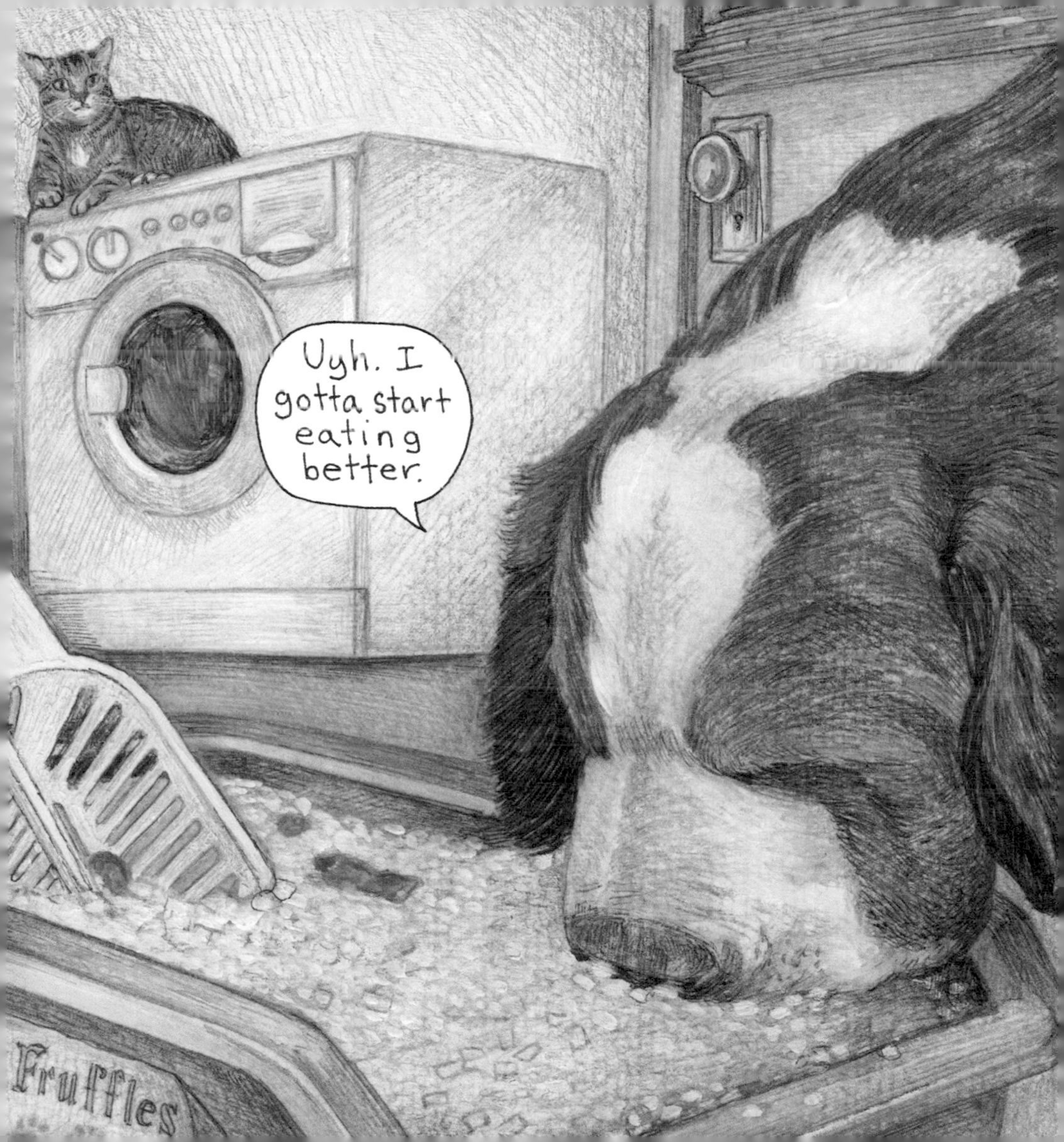
Uyh. I gotta start eating better.
Fruffles

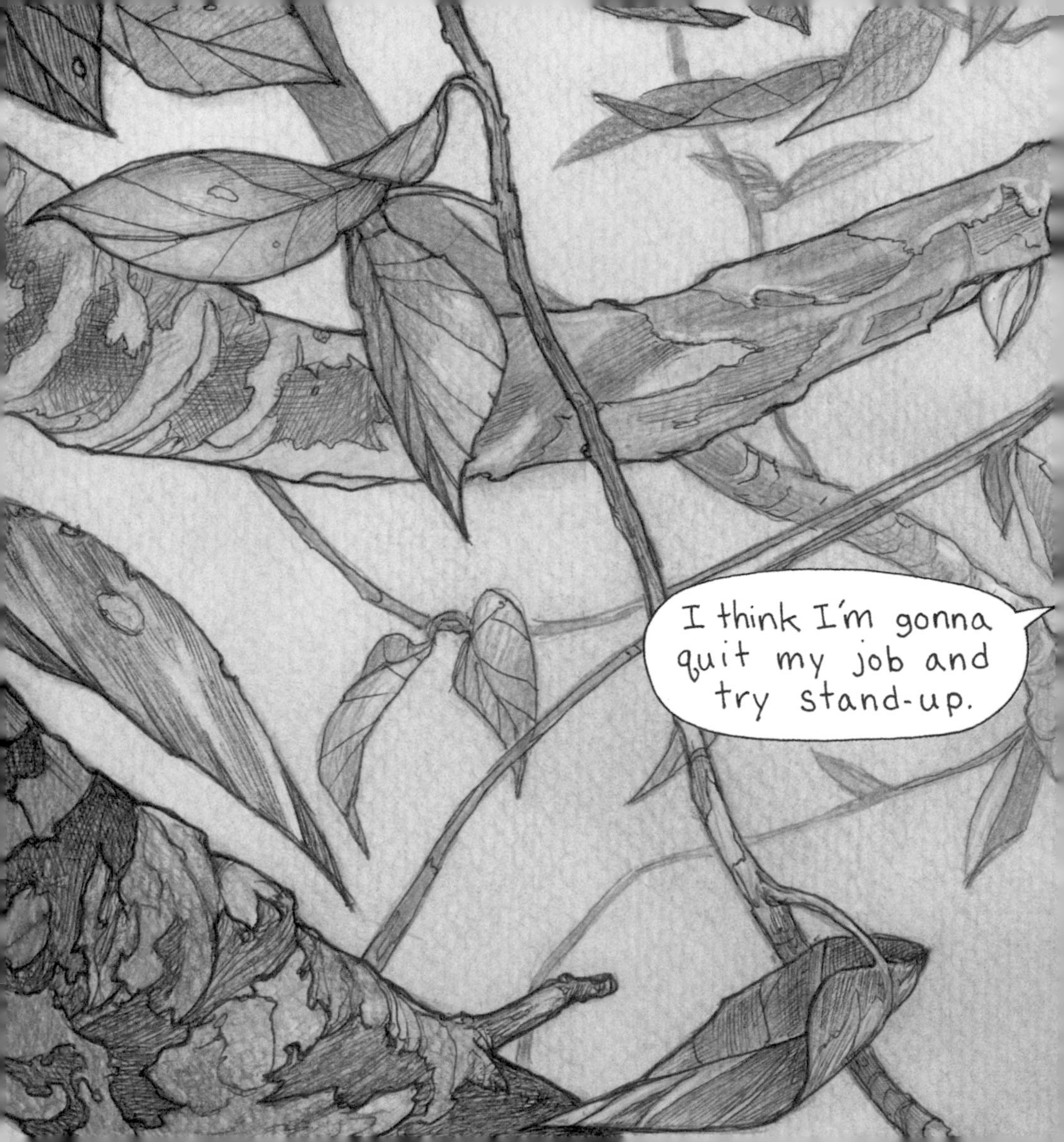
I think I'm gonna quit my job and try stand-up.

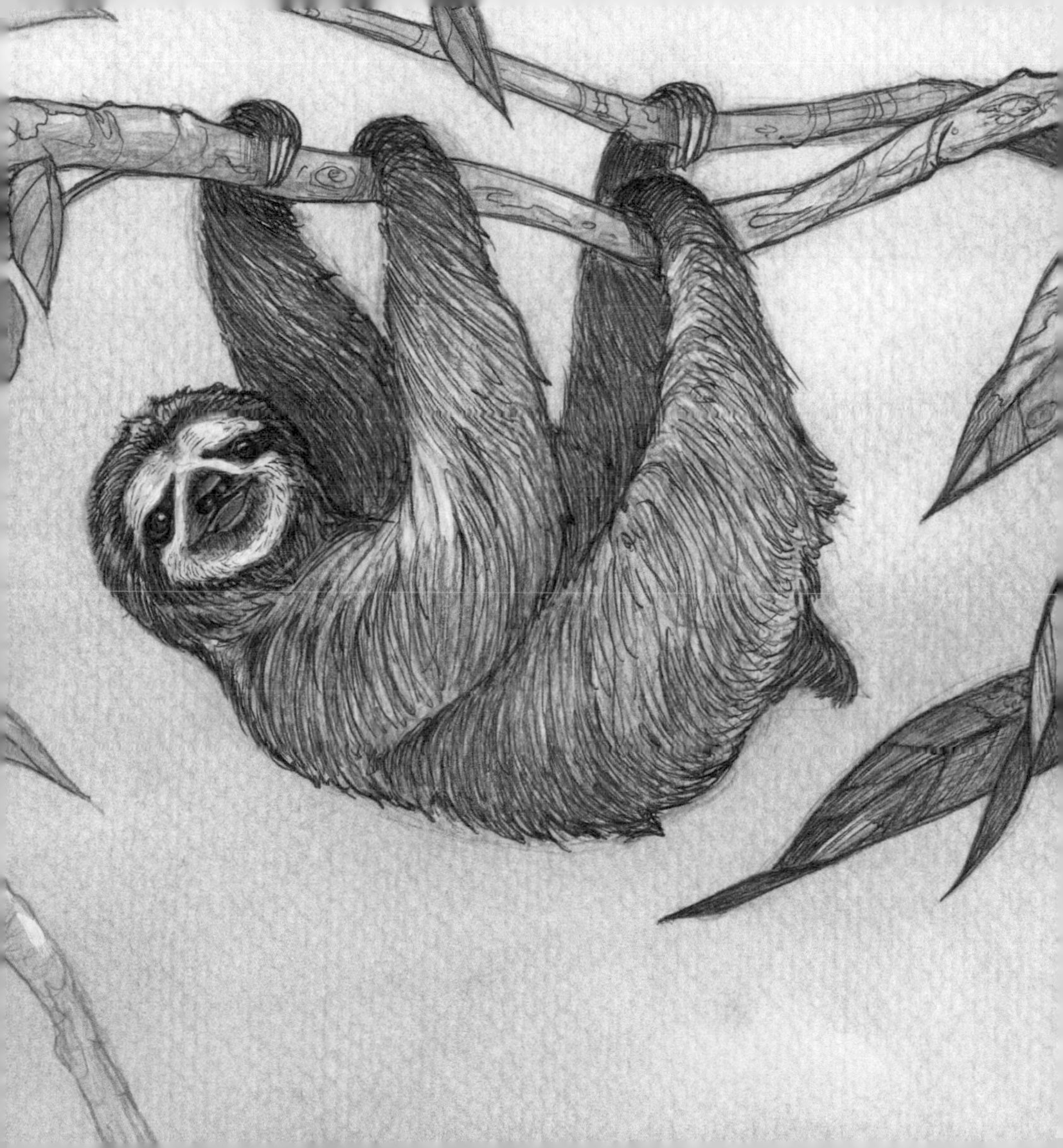

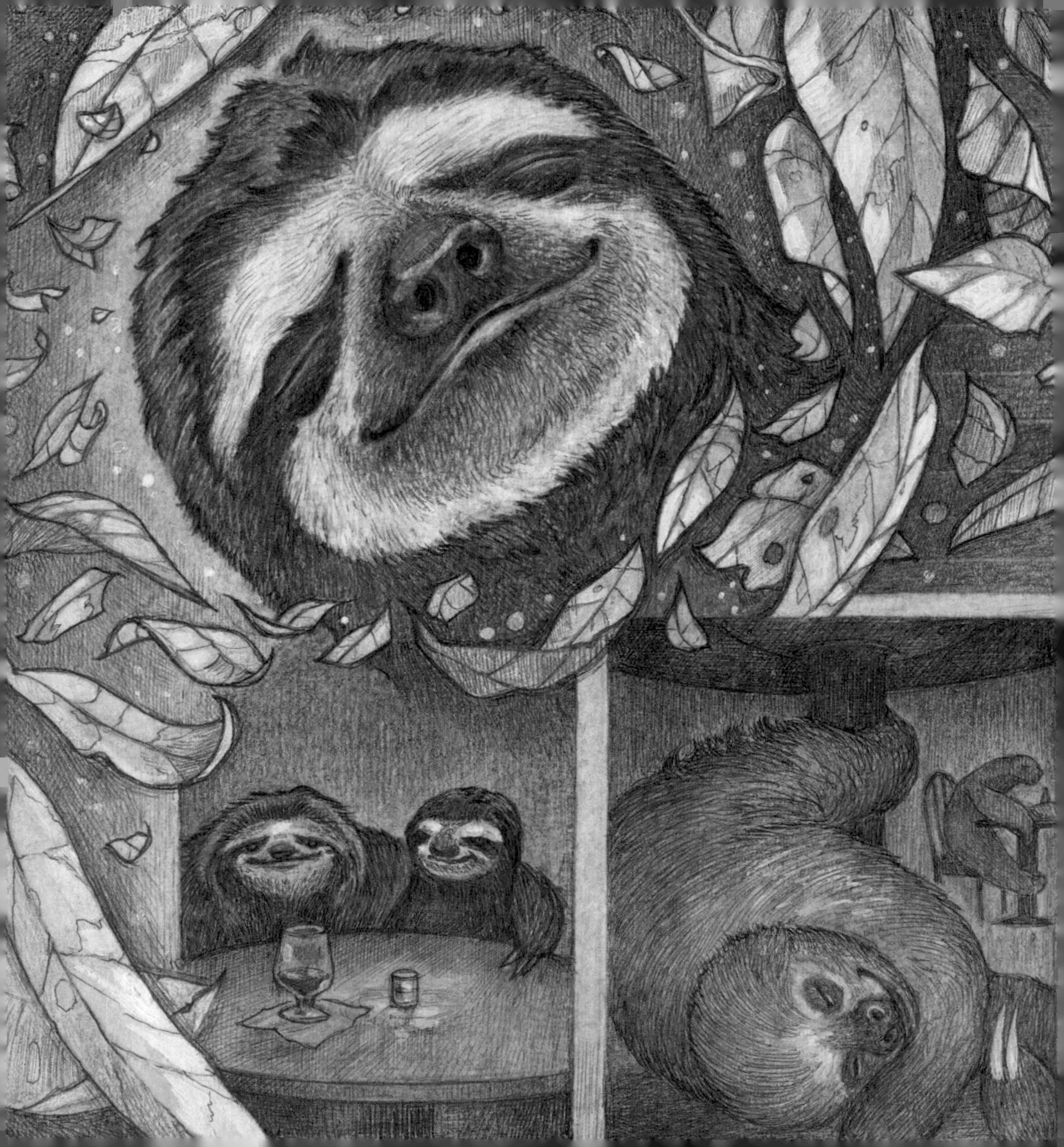

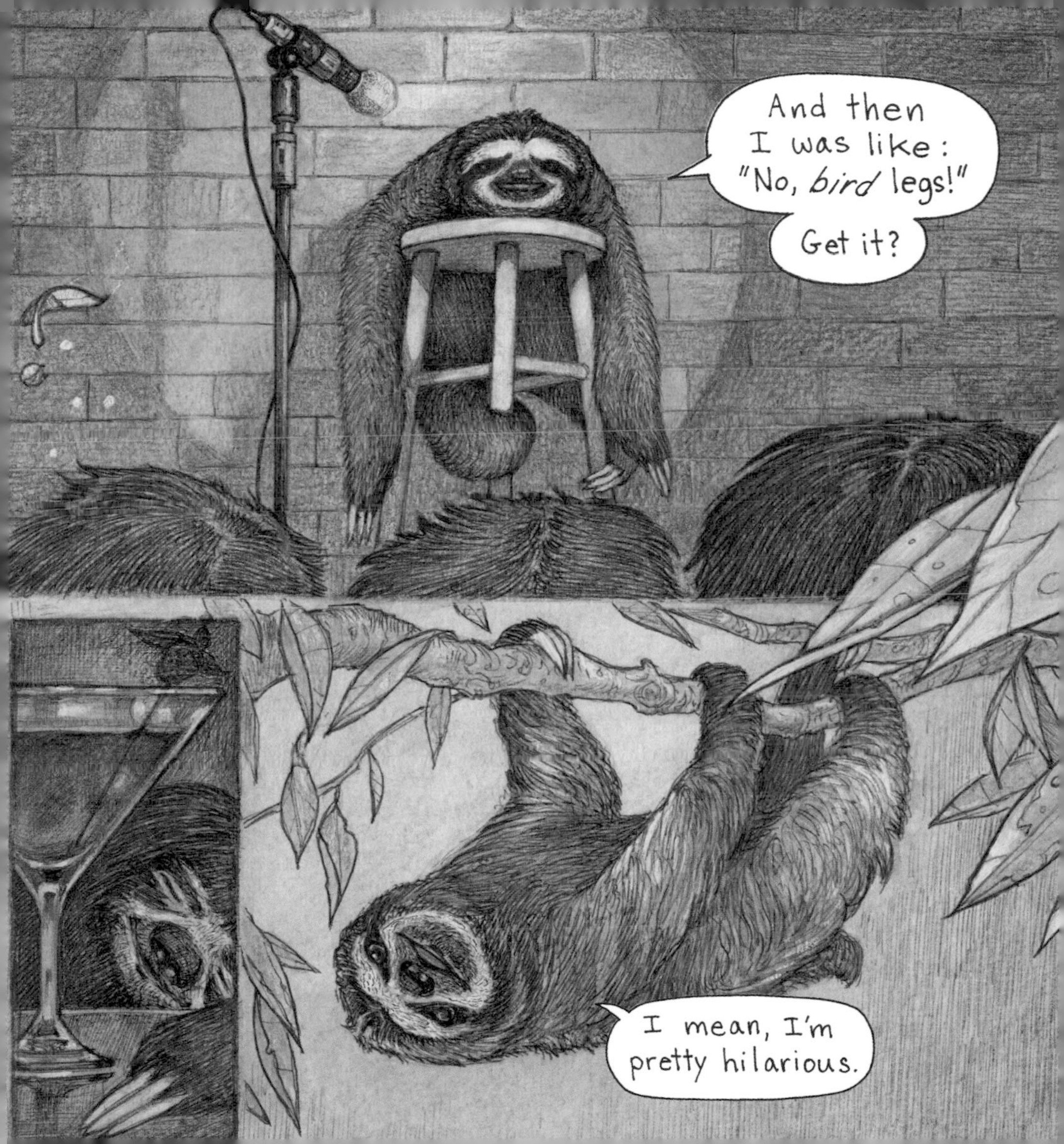
And then I was like: "No, *bird* legs!"
Get it?
I mean, I'm pretty hilarious.

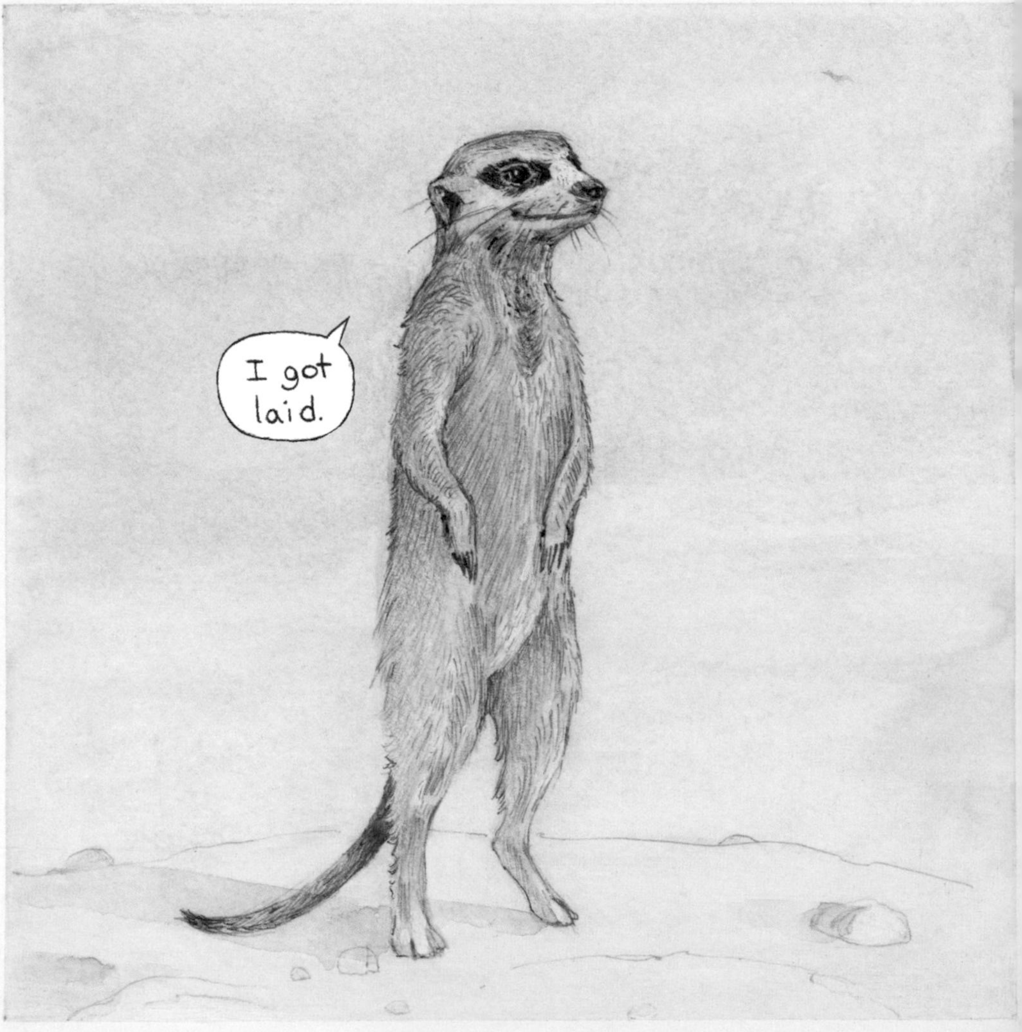
I got laid.

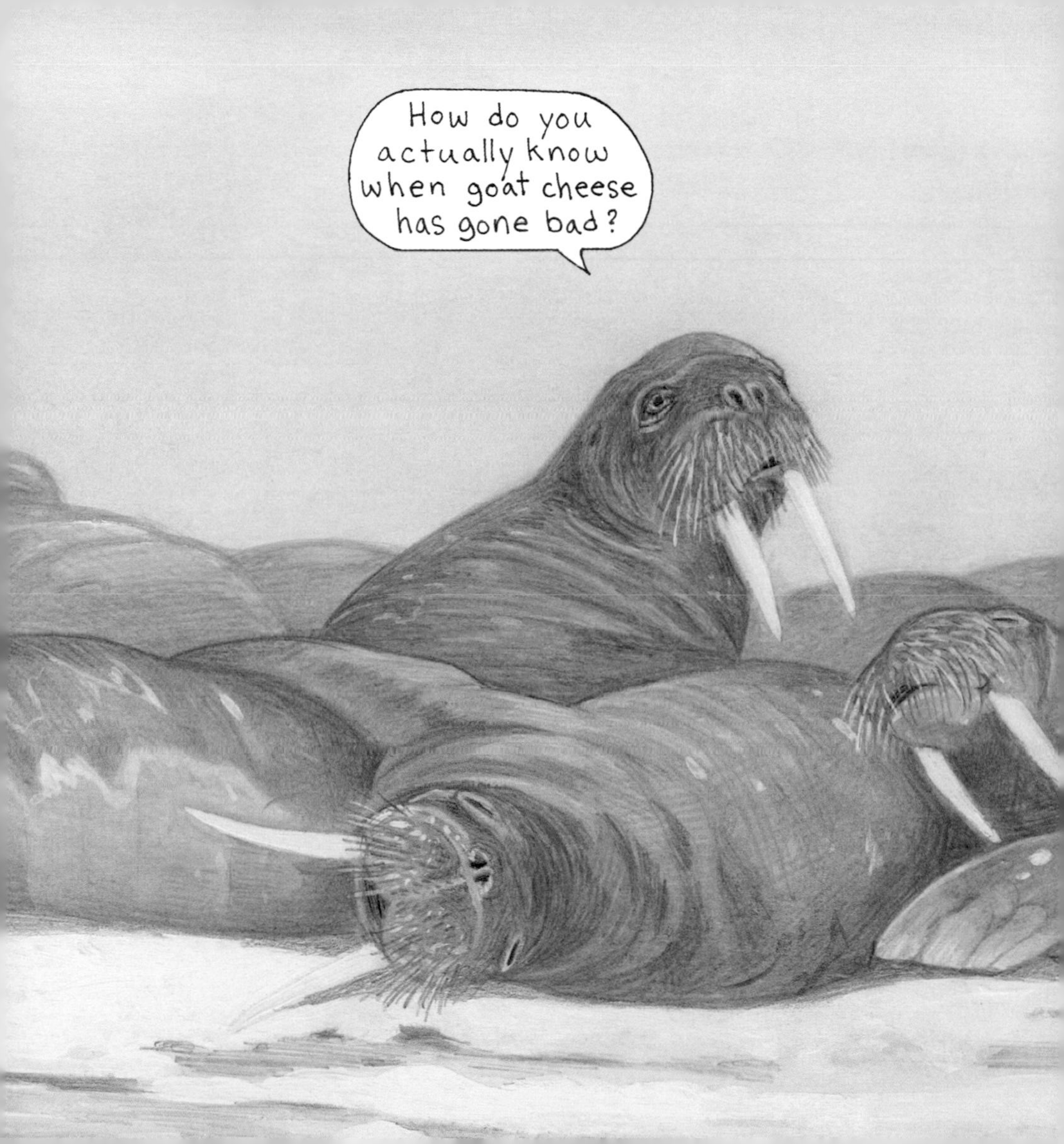
How do you actually know when goat cheese has gone bad?

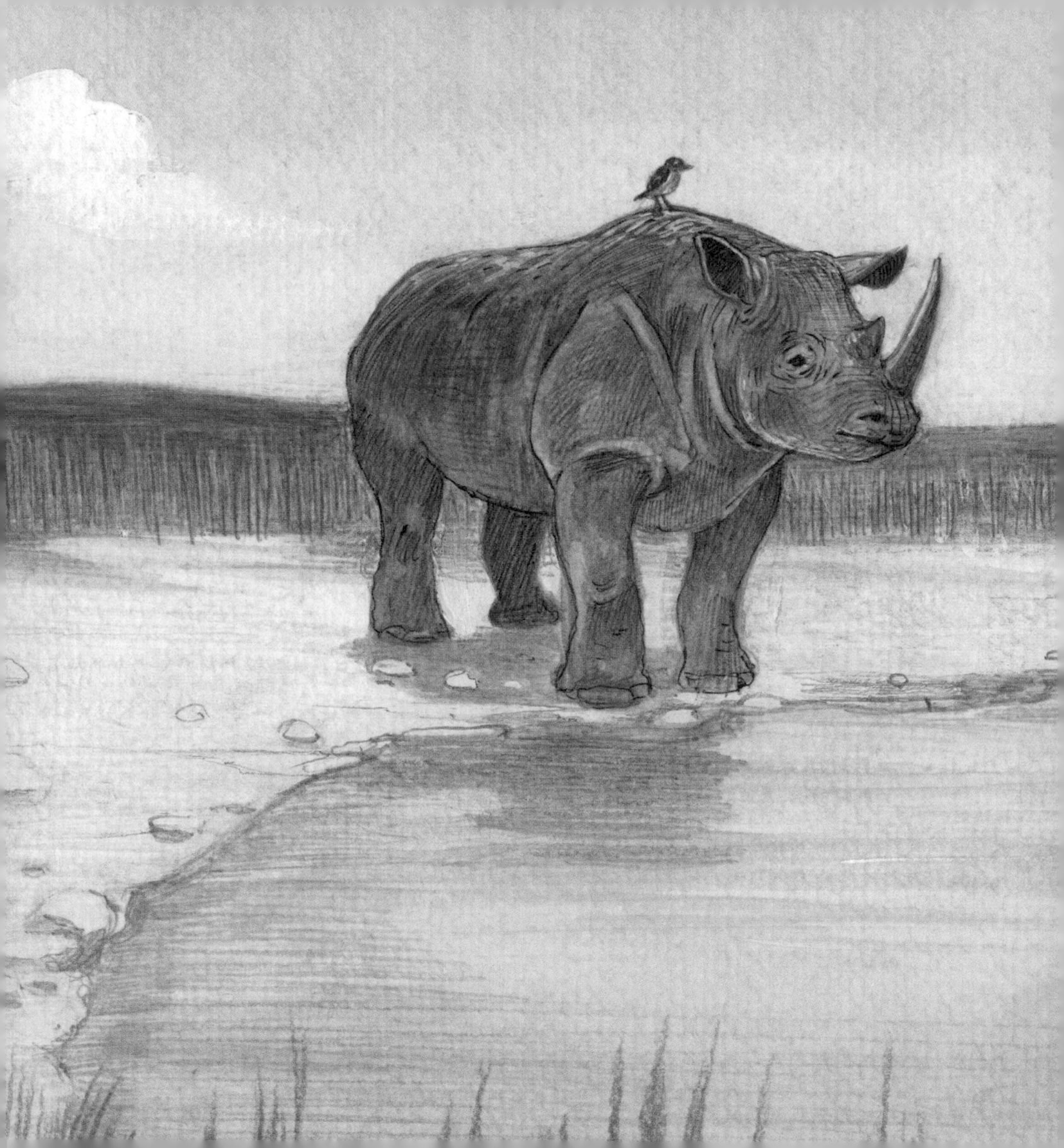

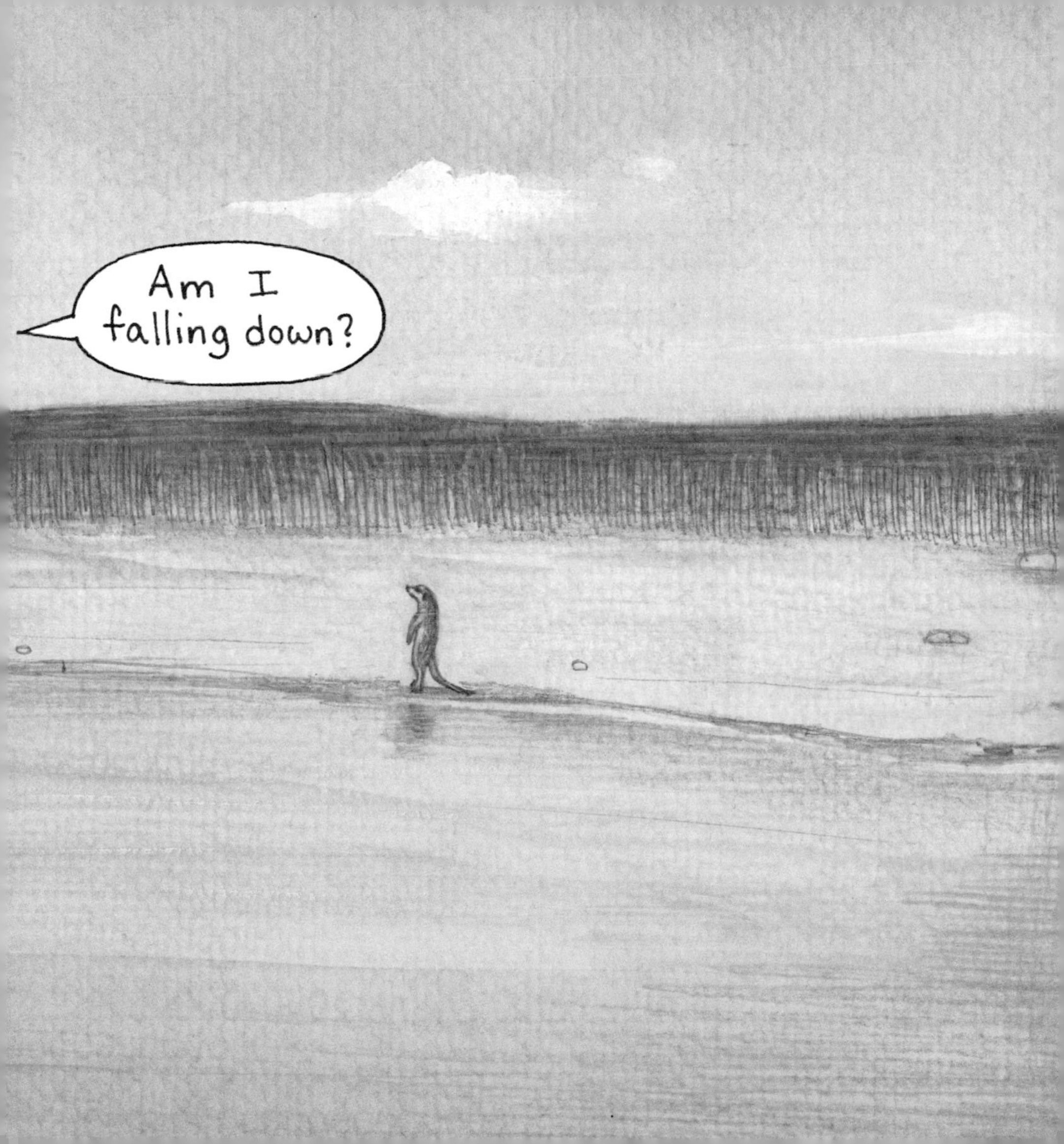
Am I falling down?

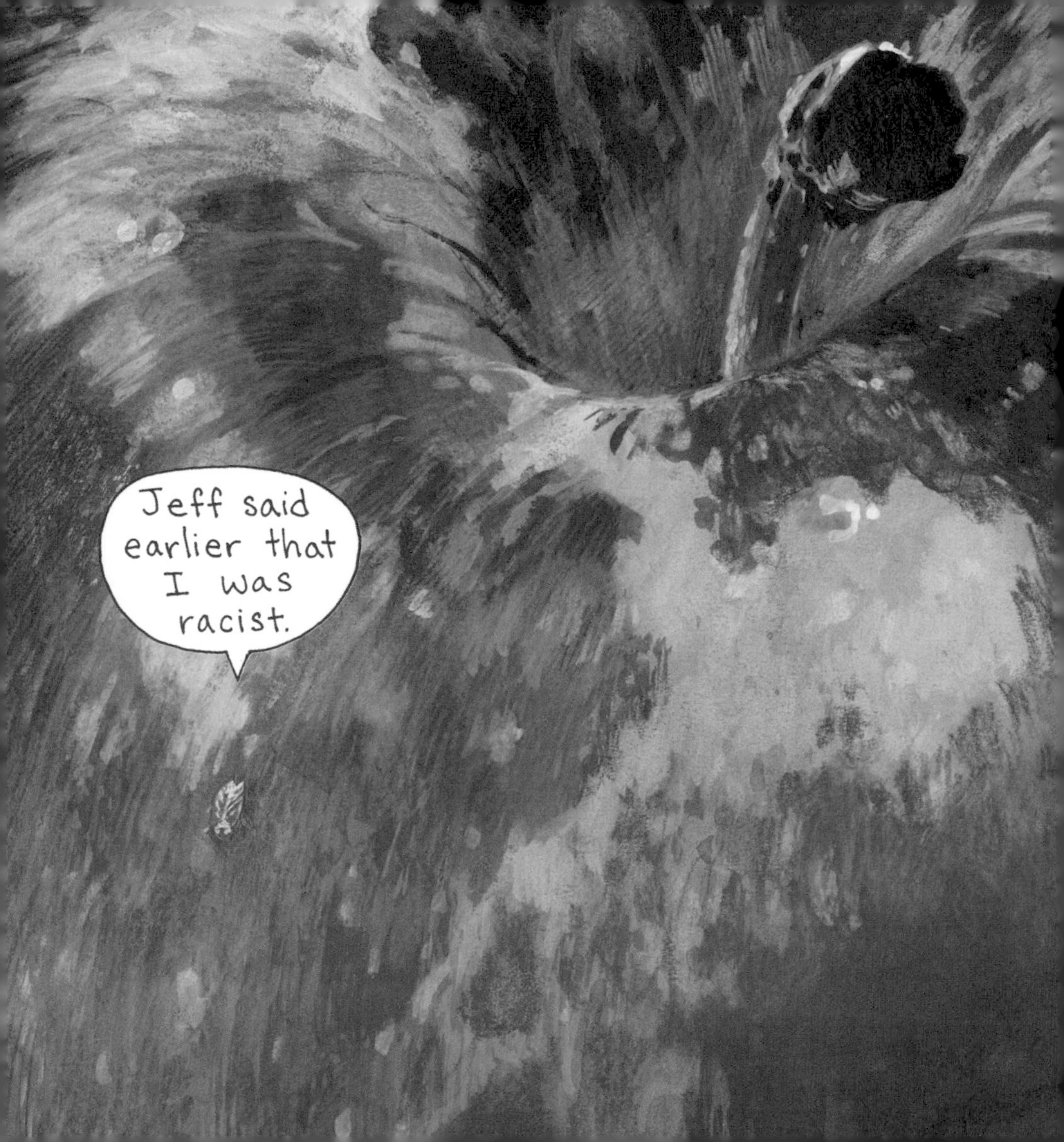
Jeff said earlier that I was racist.

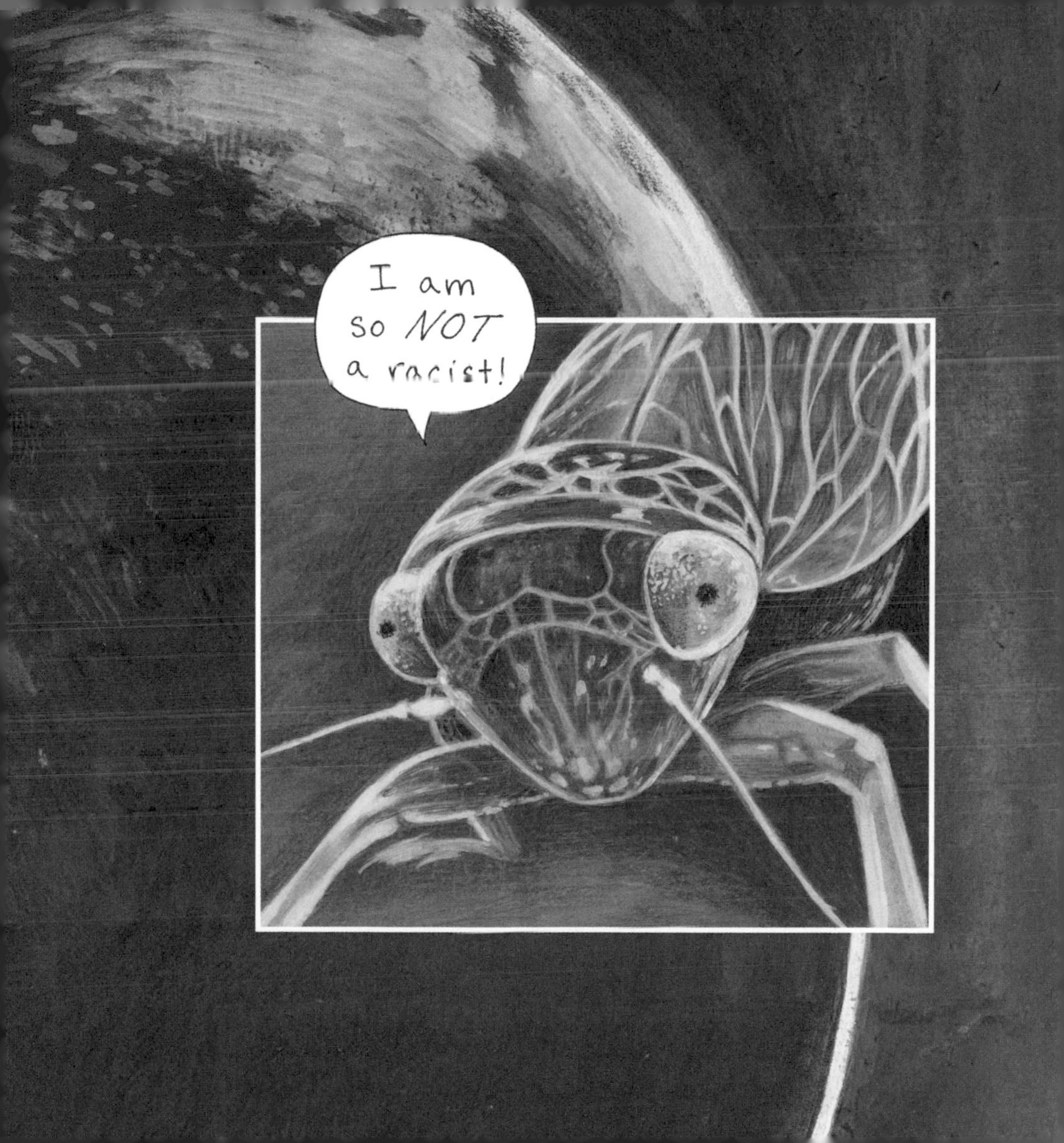
I am so NOT a racist!

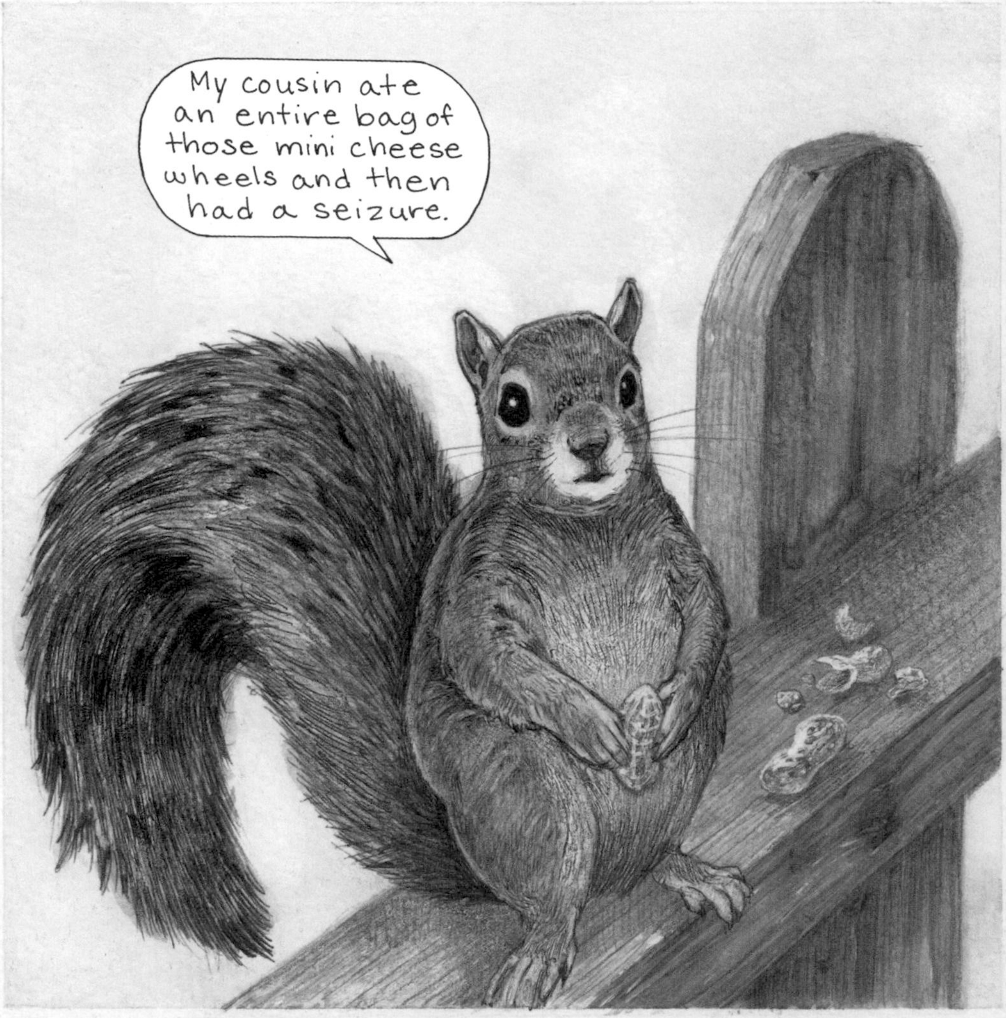
My cousin ate an entire bag of those mini cheese wheels and then had a seizure.

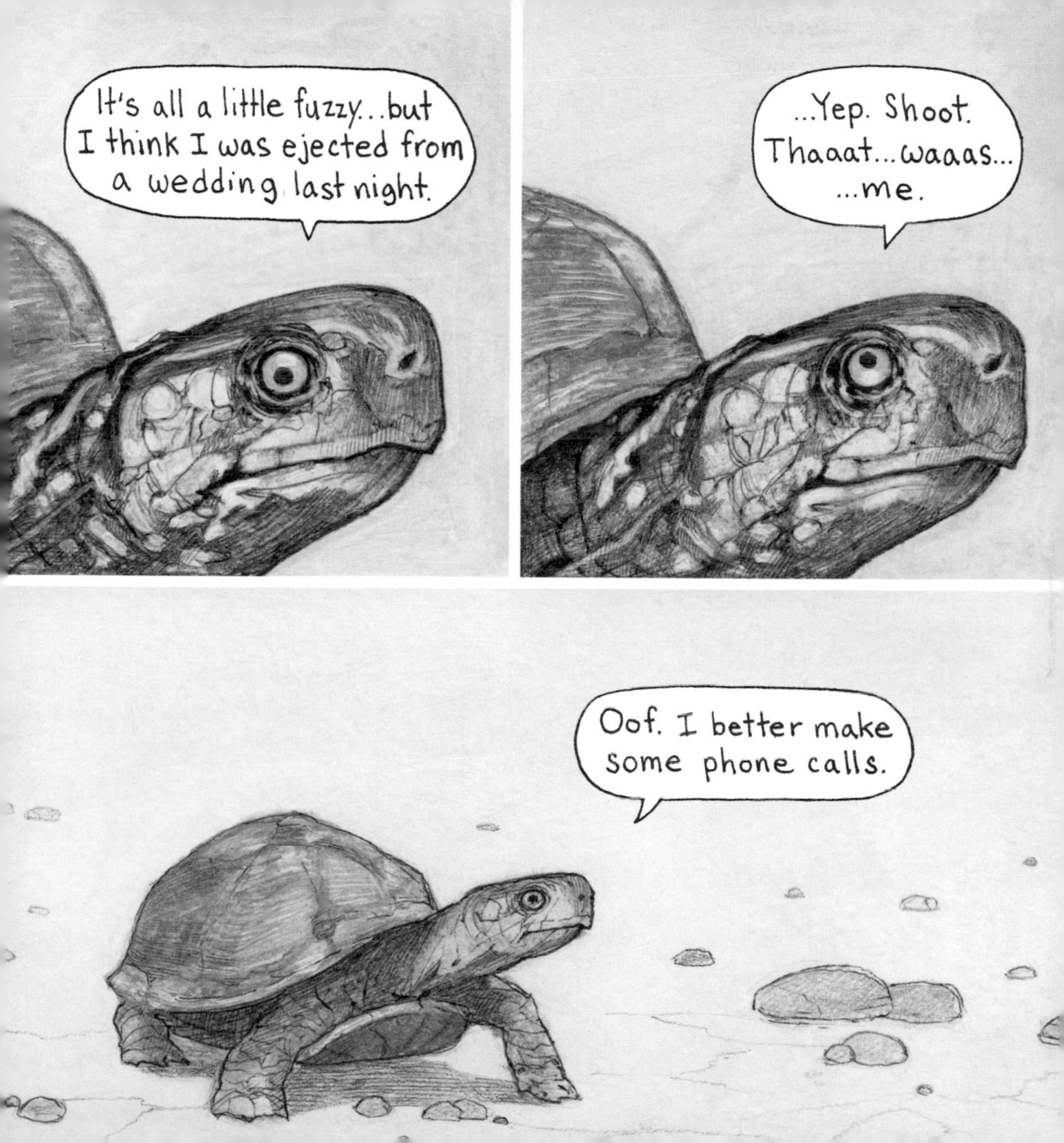
It's all a little fuzzy...but I think I was ejected from a wedding last night.
...Yep. Shoot. Thaaat...waaas... ...me.
Oof. I better make some phone calls.

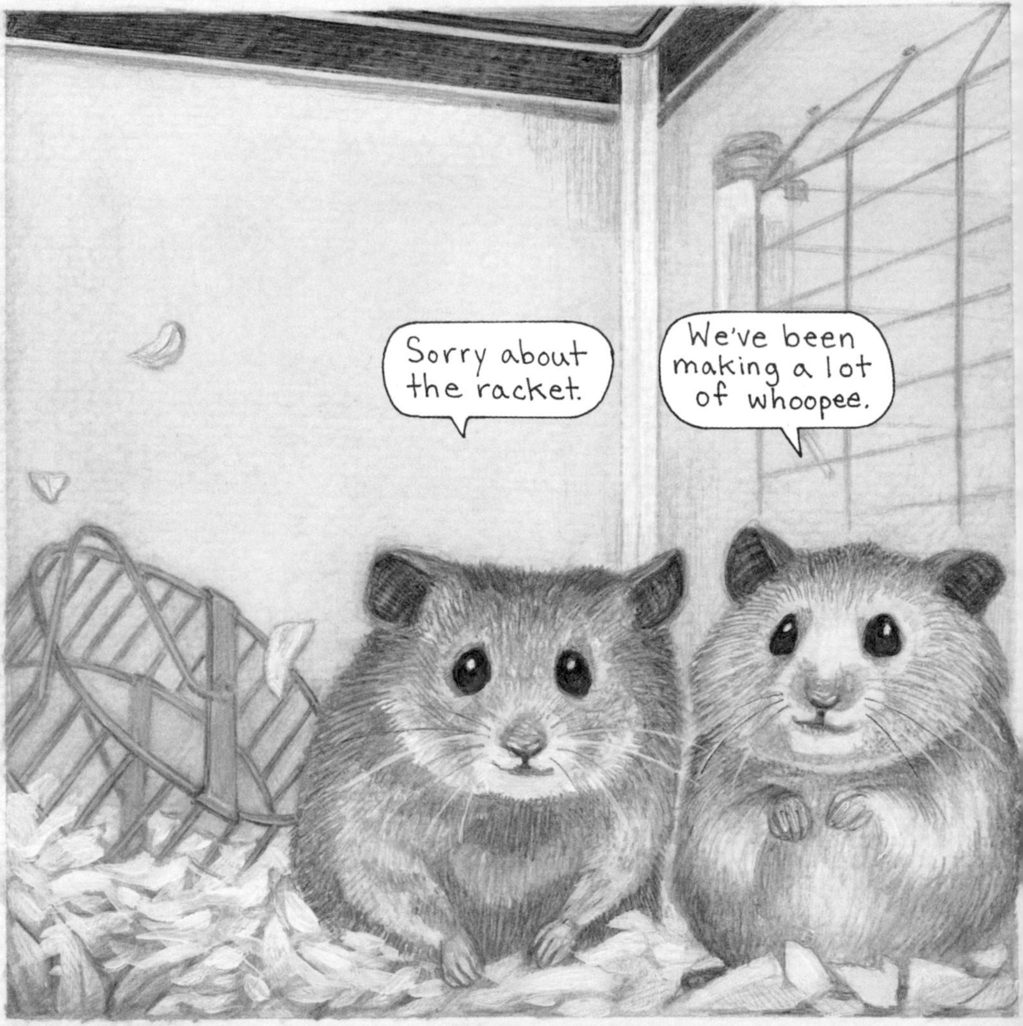
Sorry about the racket.
We've been making a lot of whoopee.

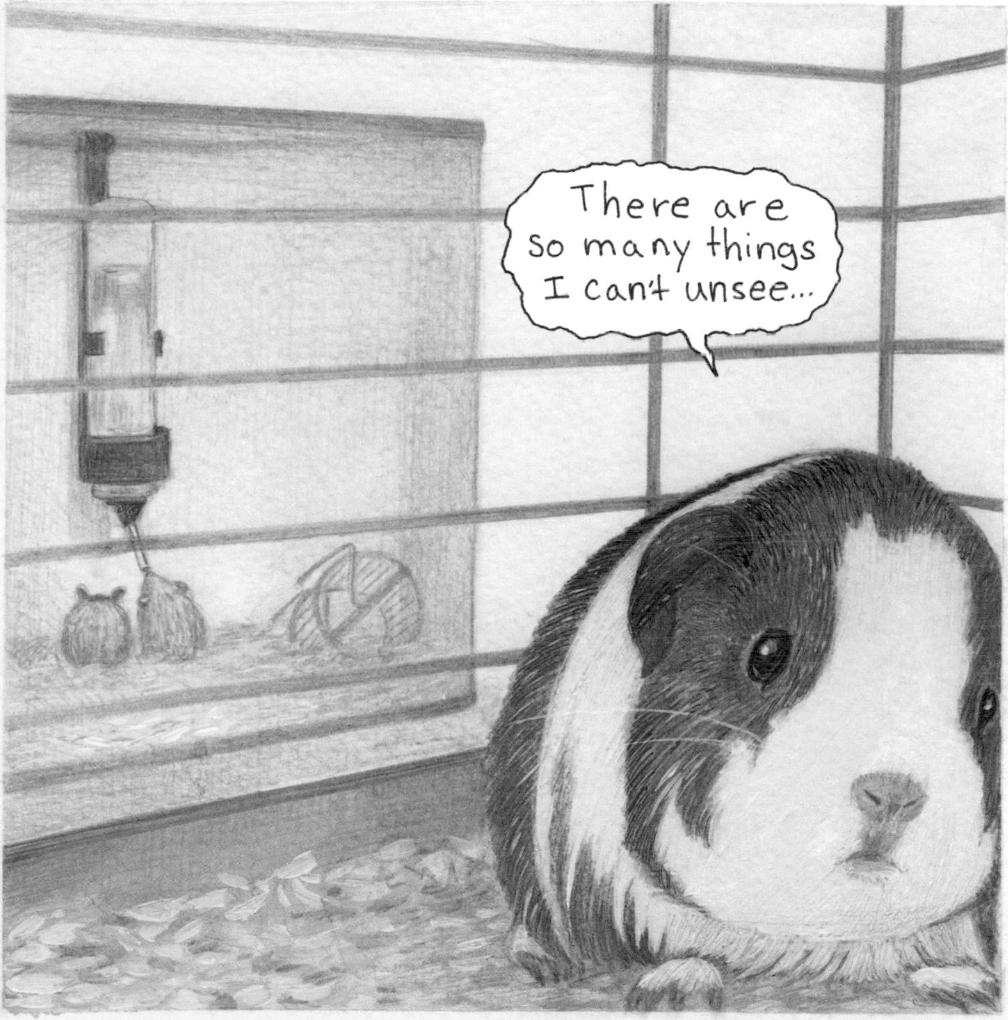
There are so many things I can't unsee...

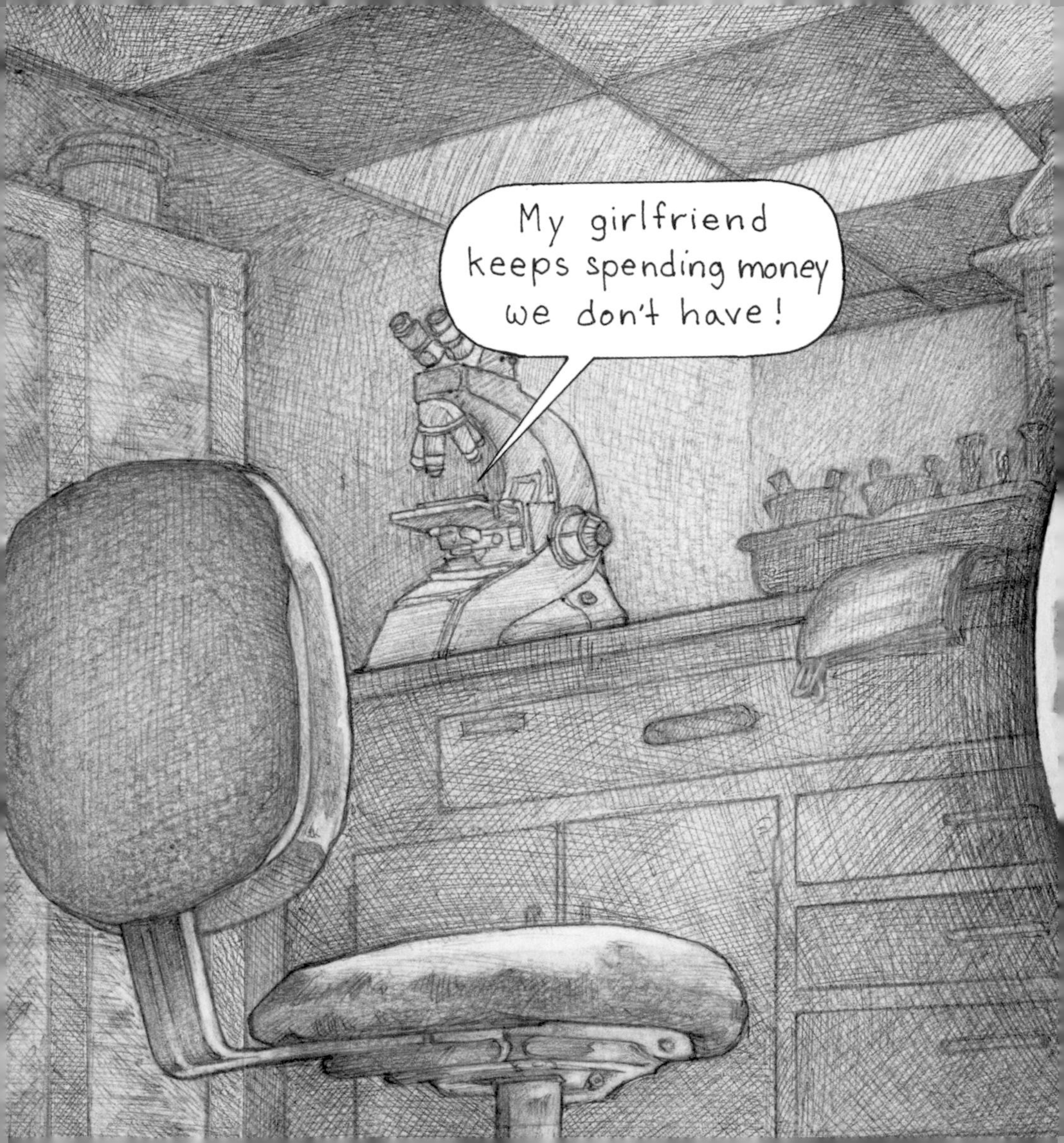
My girlfriend keeps spending money we don't have!

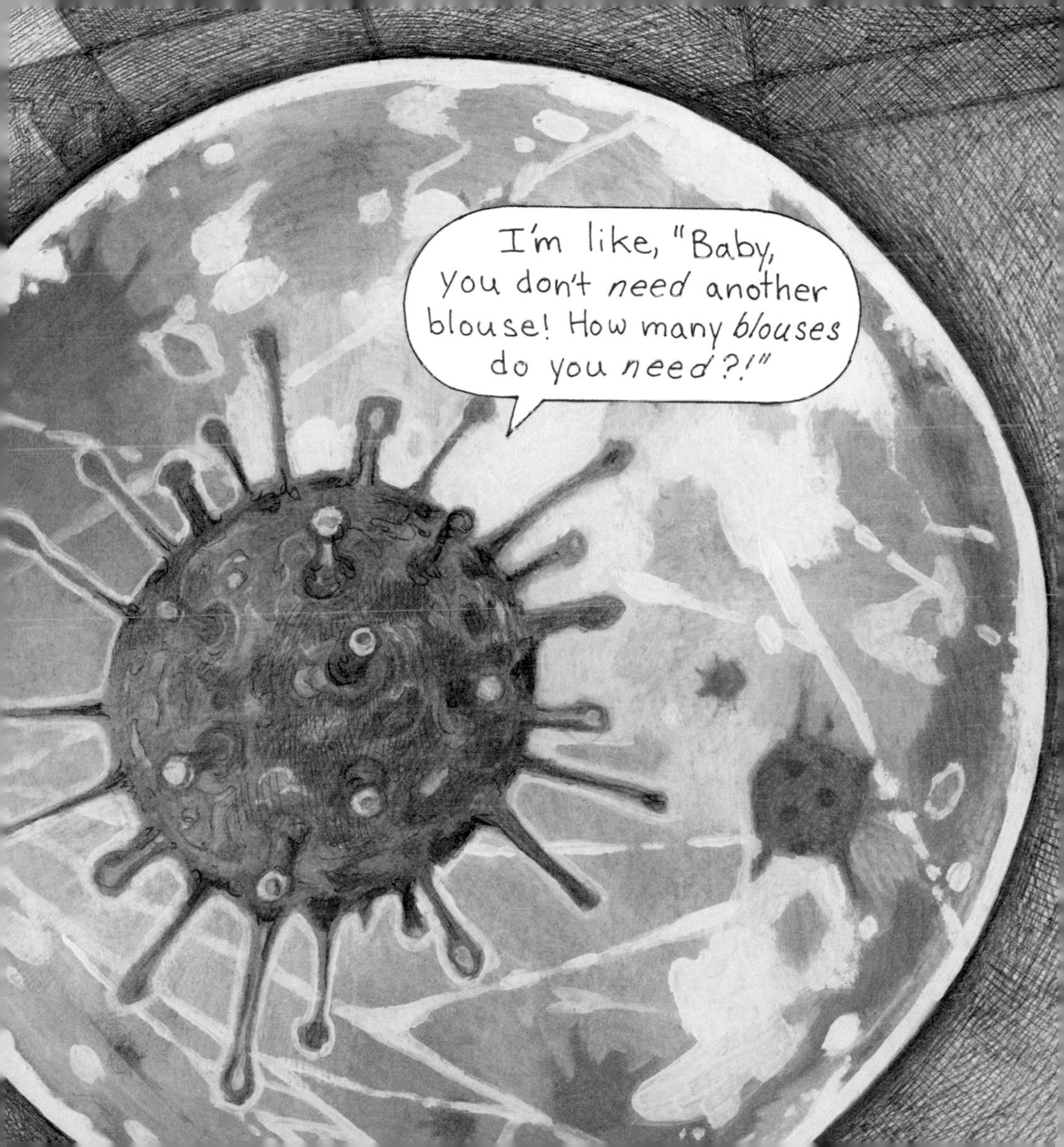
I'm like, "Baby, you don't *need* another blouse! How many *blouses* do you *need*?!"

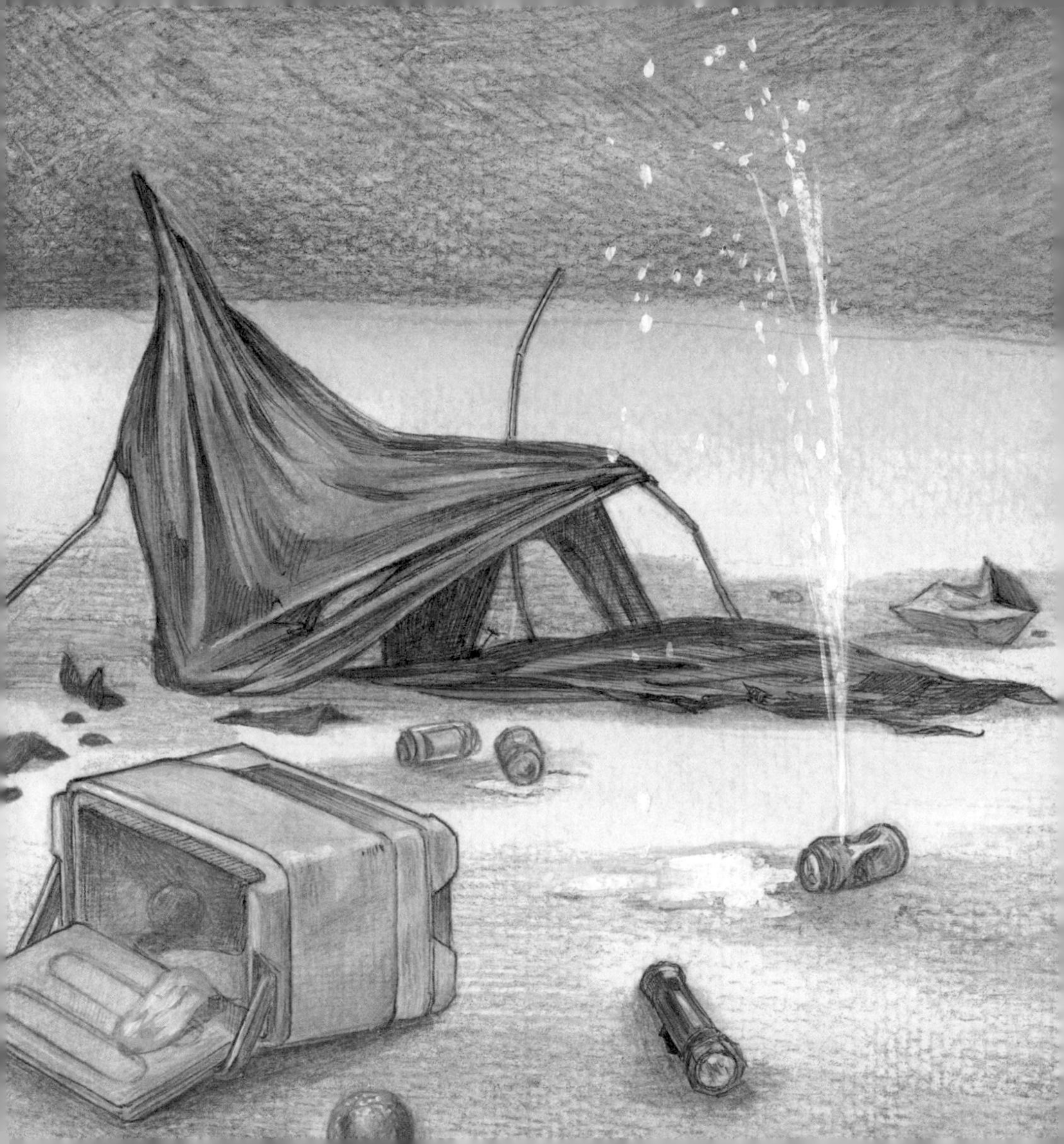

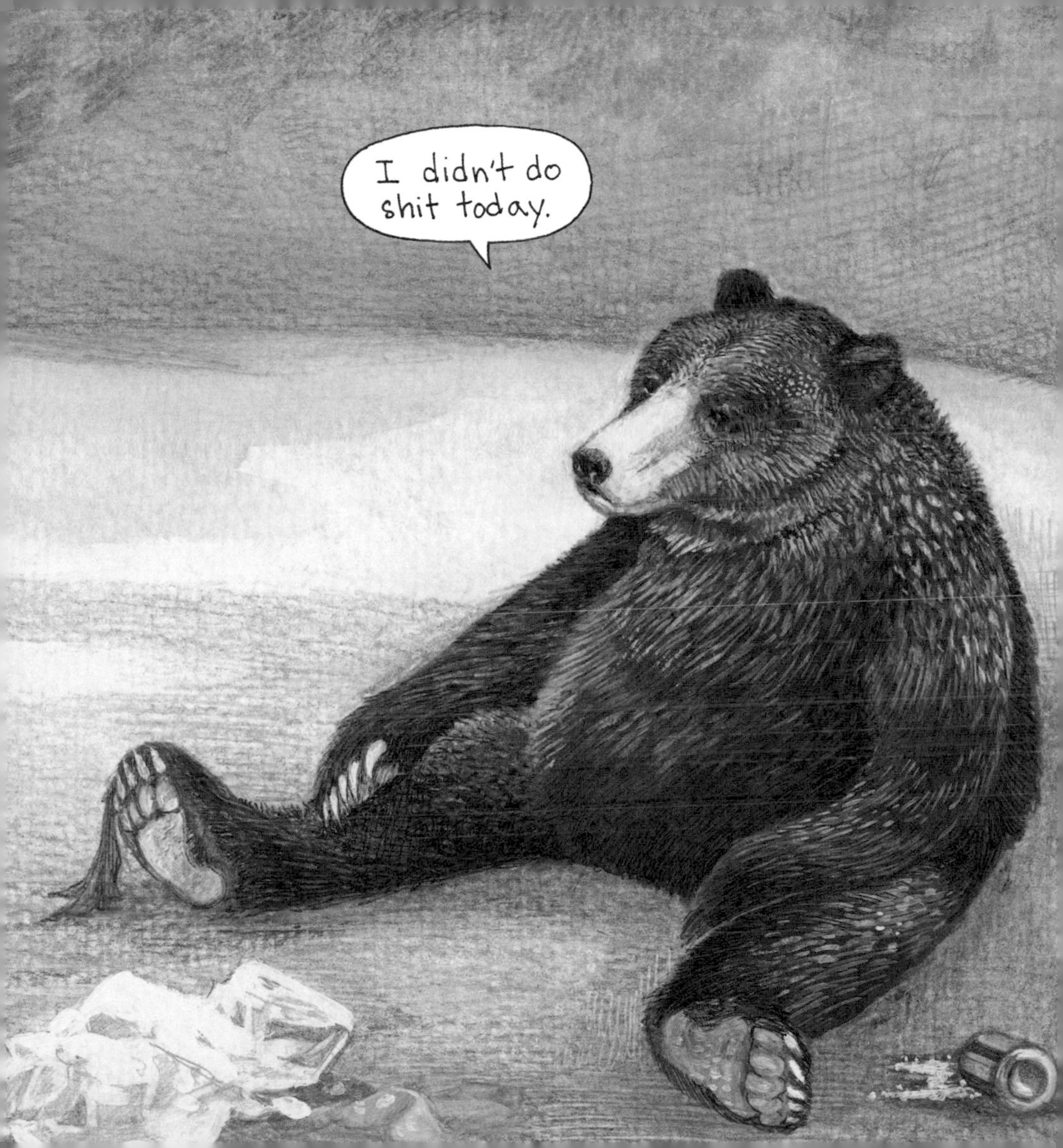
I didn't do shit today.

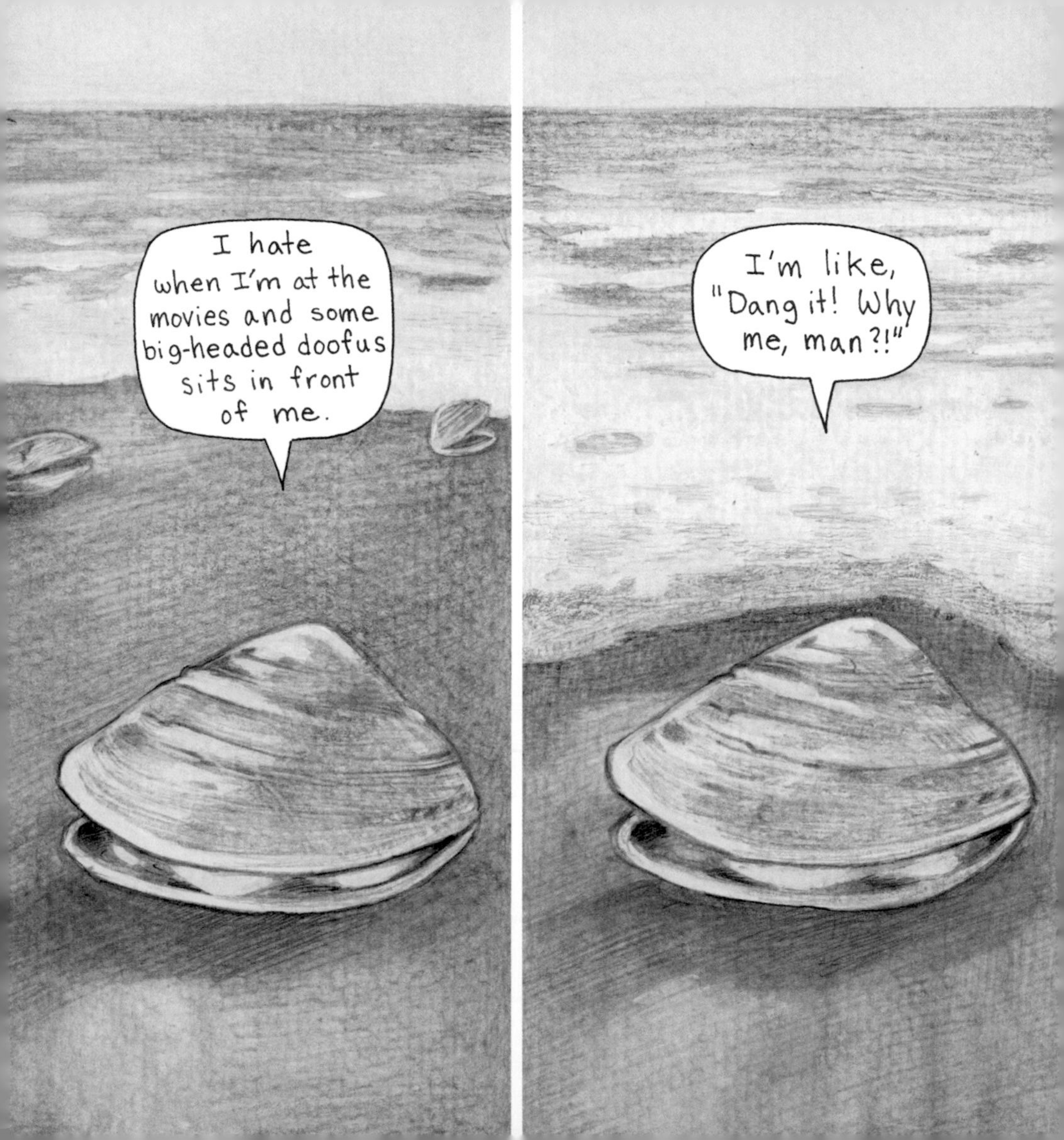
I hate when I'm at the movies and some big-headed doofus sits in front of me.
I'm like, "Dang it! Why me, man?!"

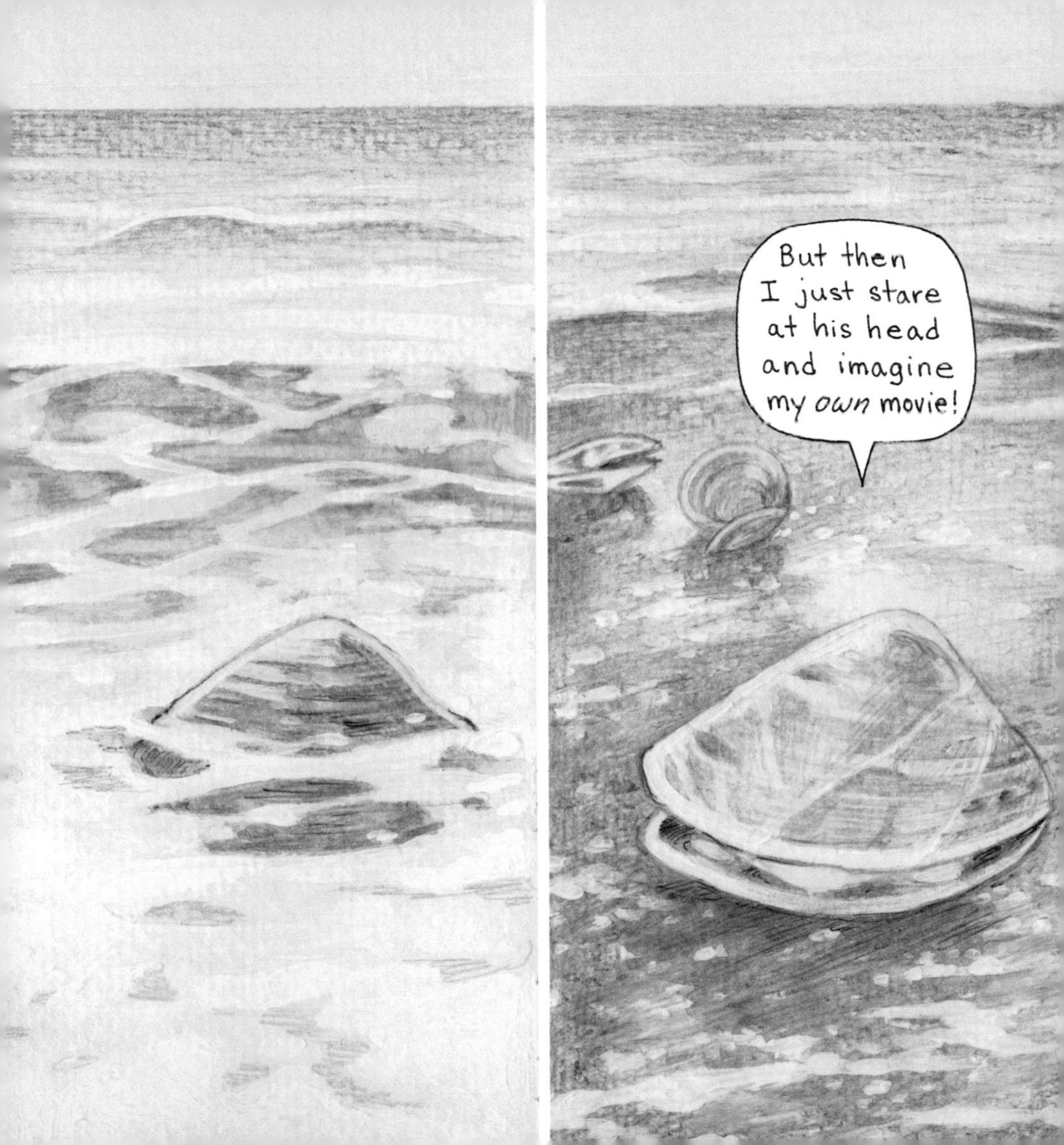
But then I just stare at his head and imagine my *own* movie!

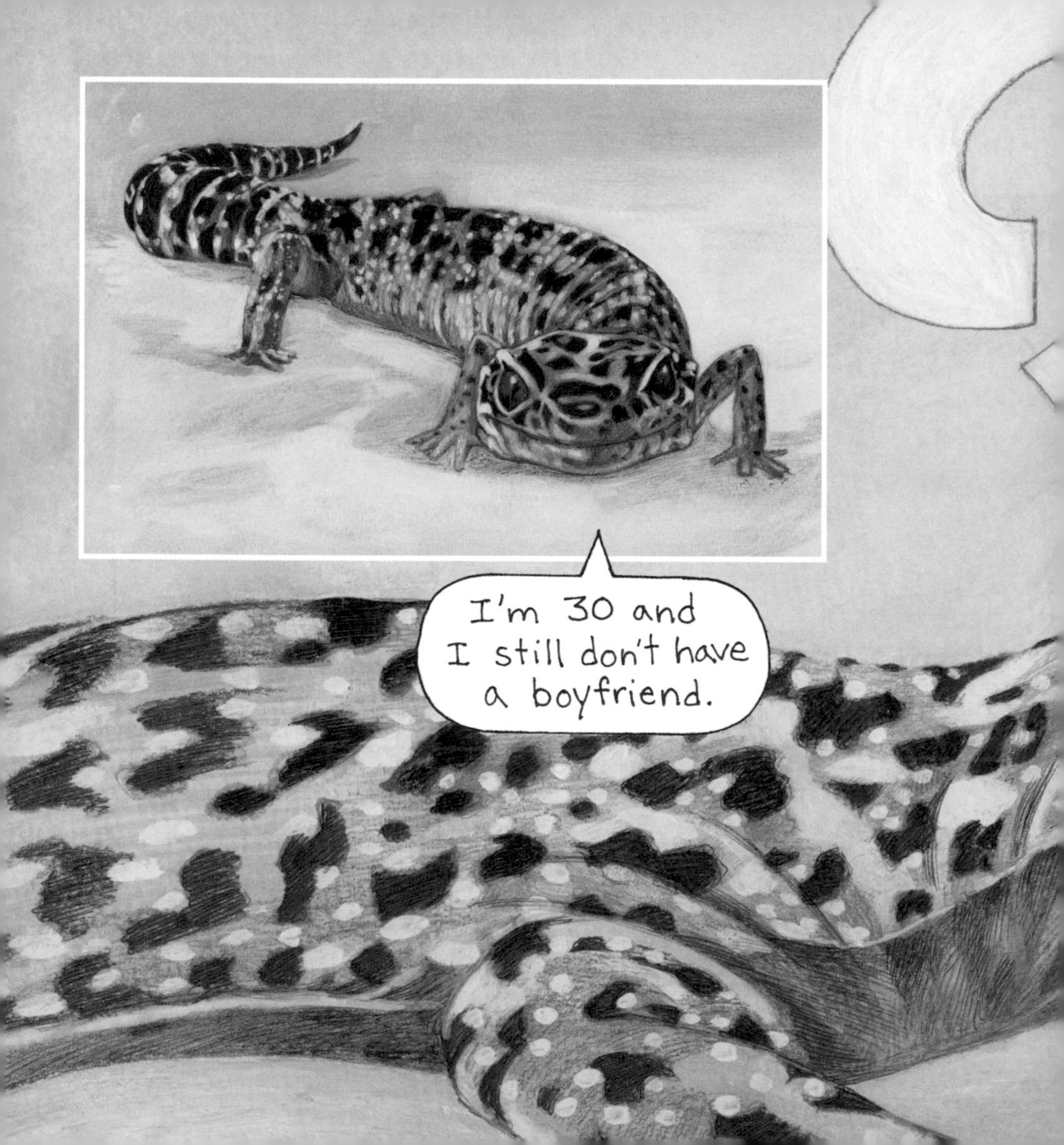
I'm 30 and I still don't have a boyfriend.

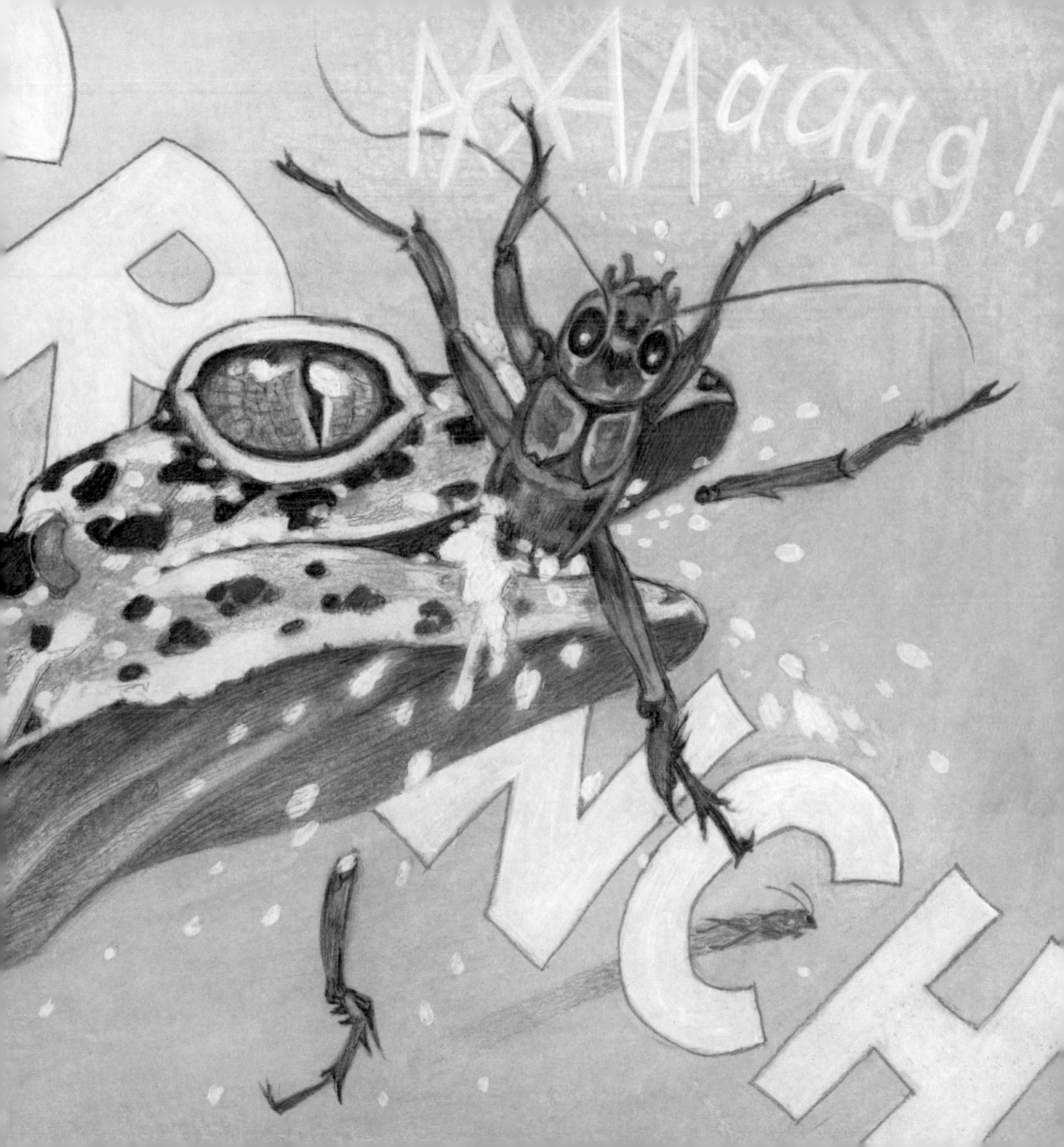
AAAAaaaag!!

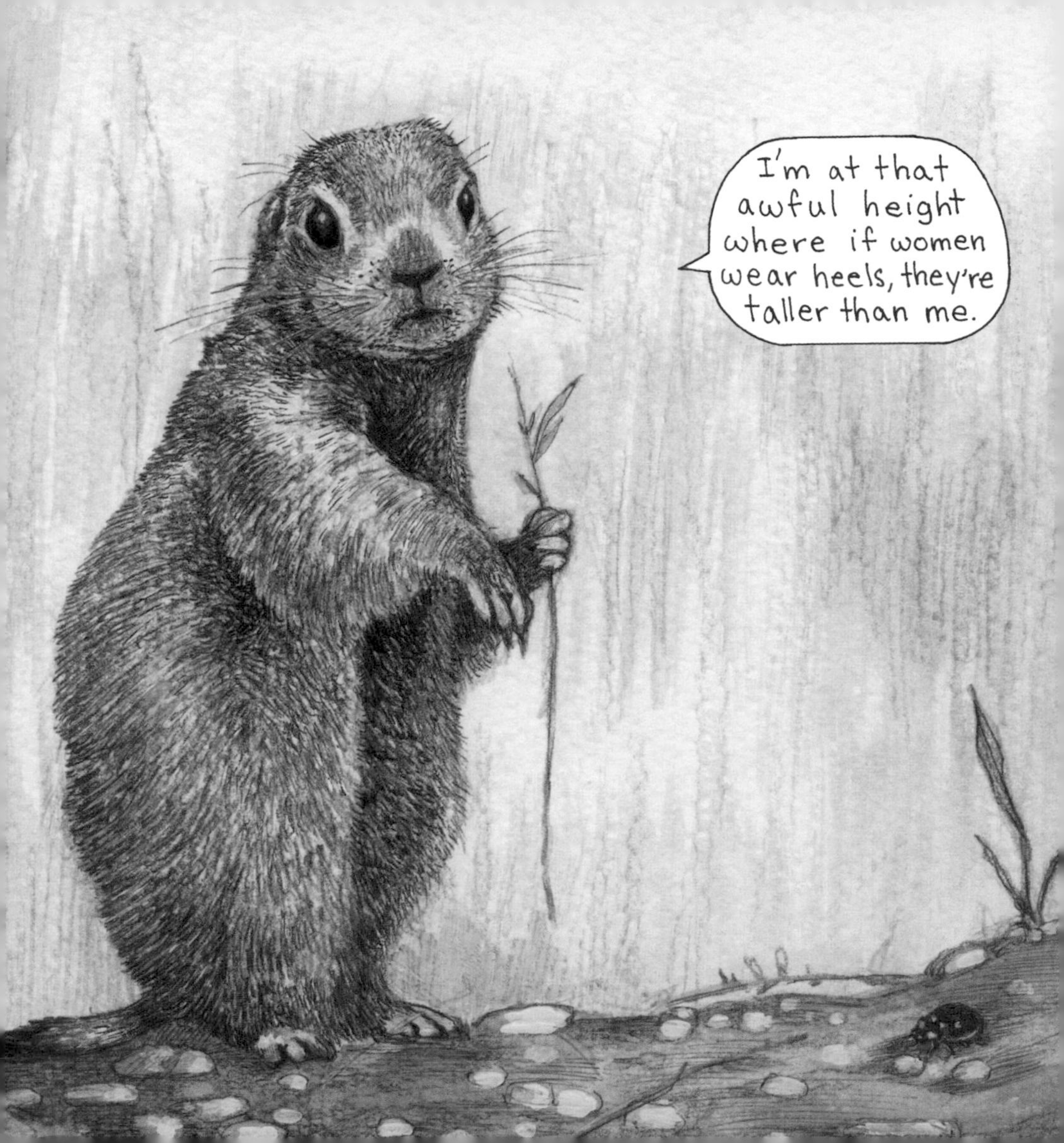
I'm at that awful height where if women wear heels, they're taller than me.

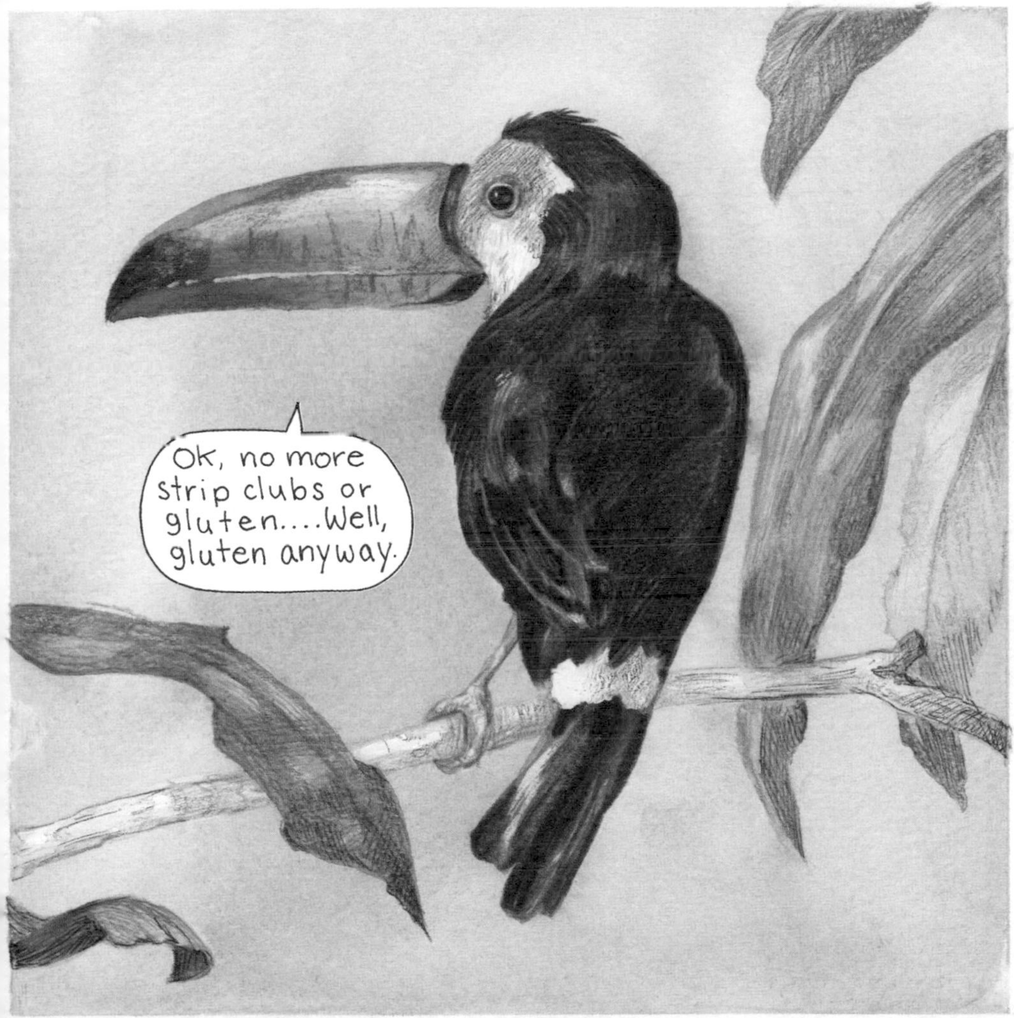
Ok, no more strip clubs or gluten....Well, gluten anyway.

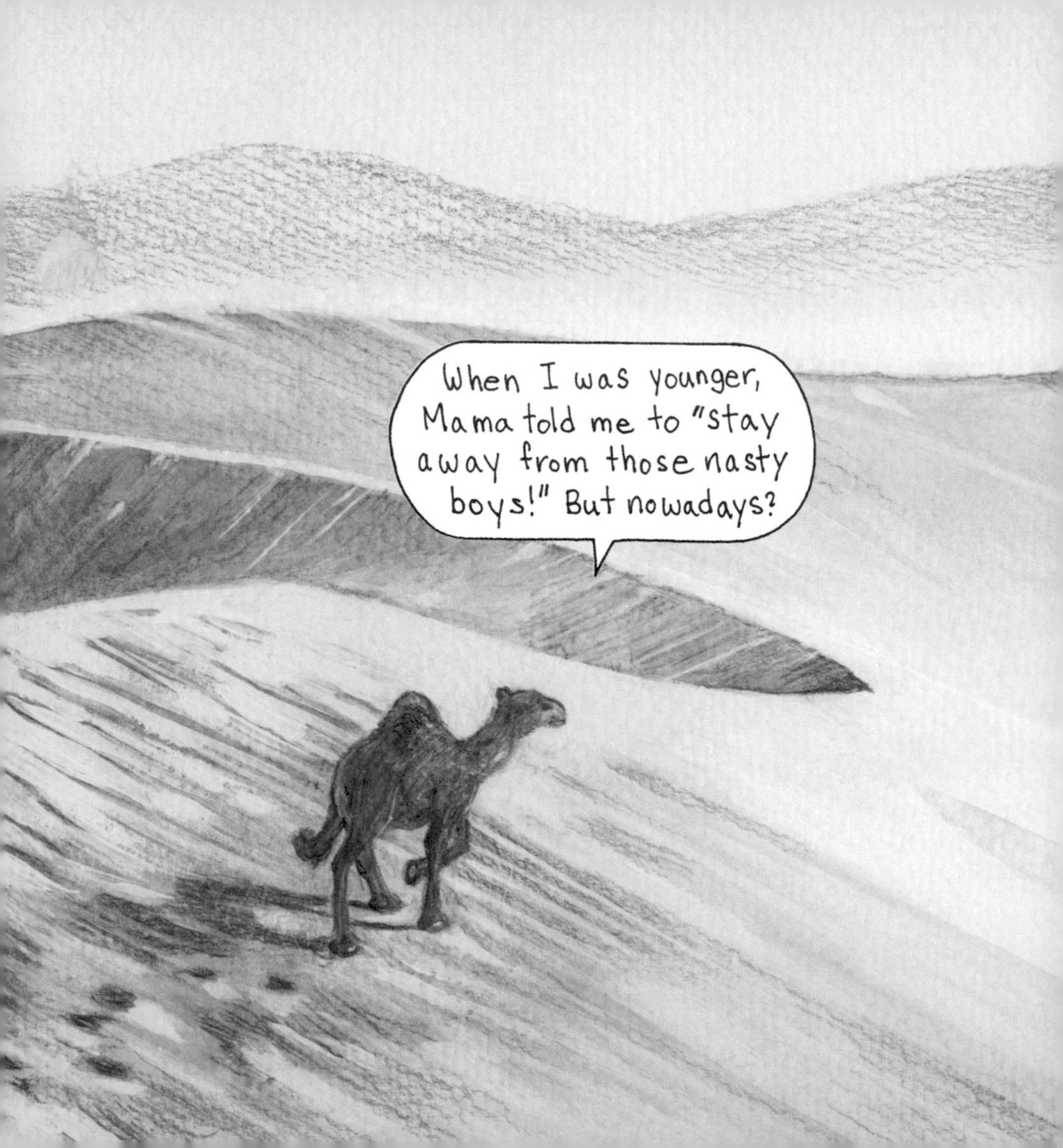
When I was younger, Mama told me to "stay away from those nasty boys!" But nowadays?

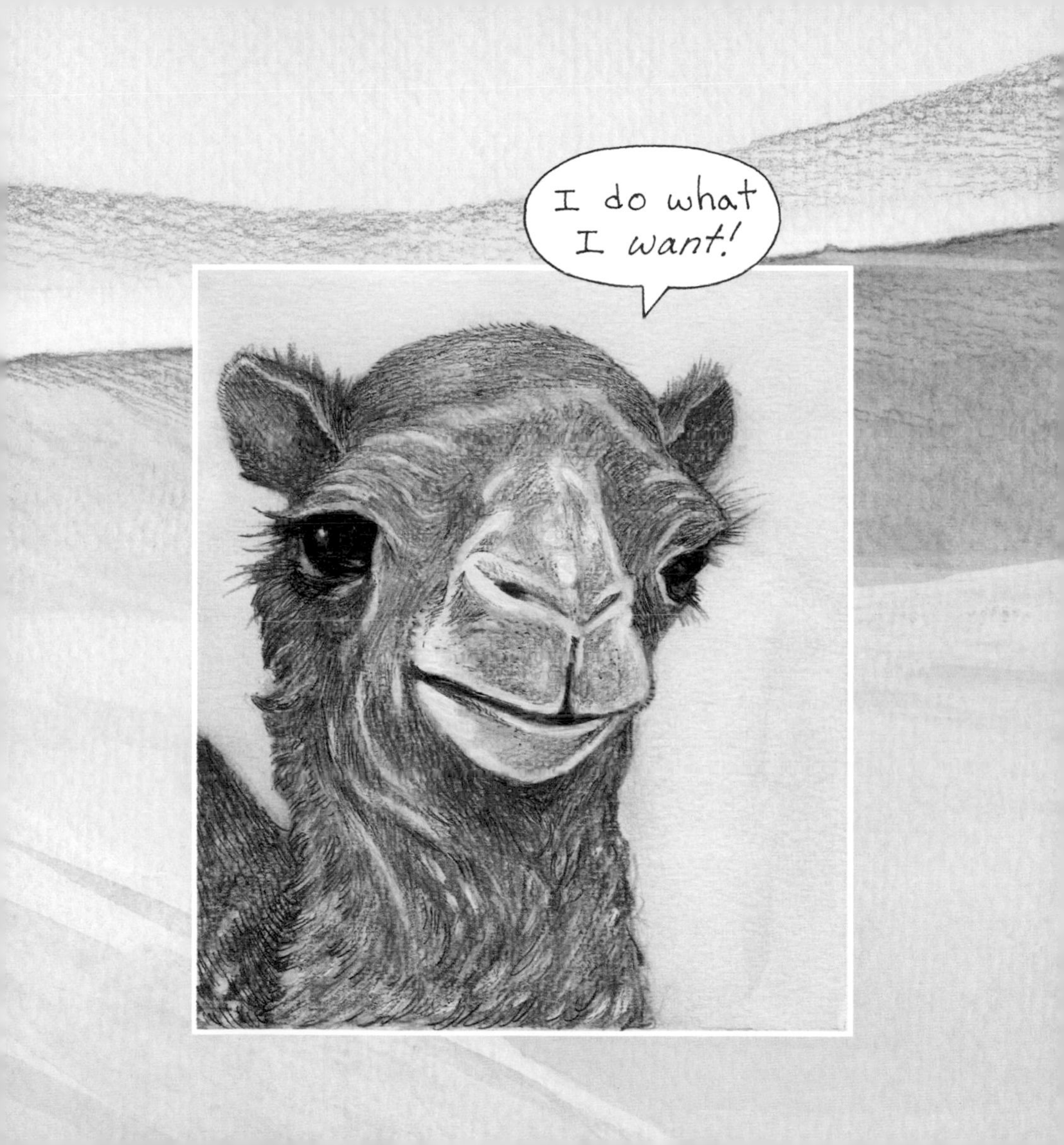
I do what I want!

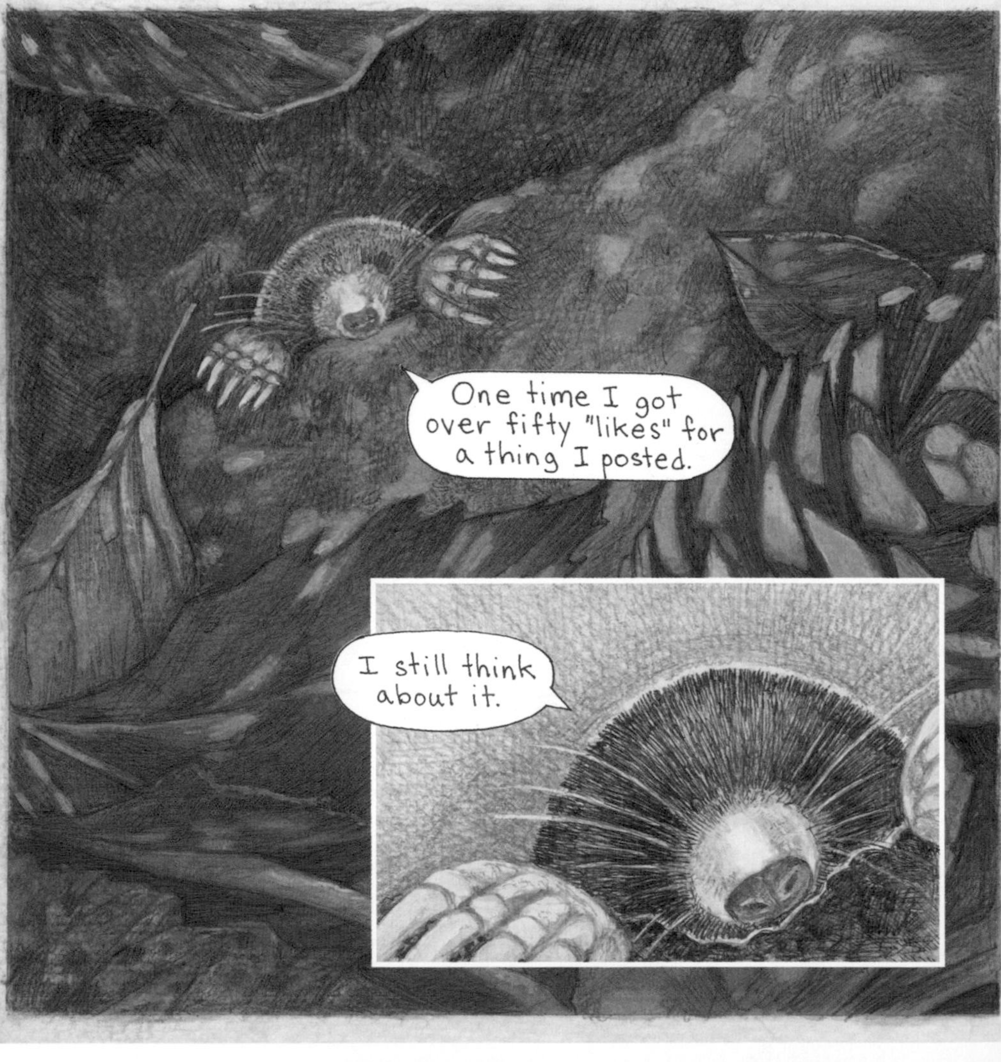
One time I got over fifty "likes" for a thing I posted.
I still think about it.

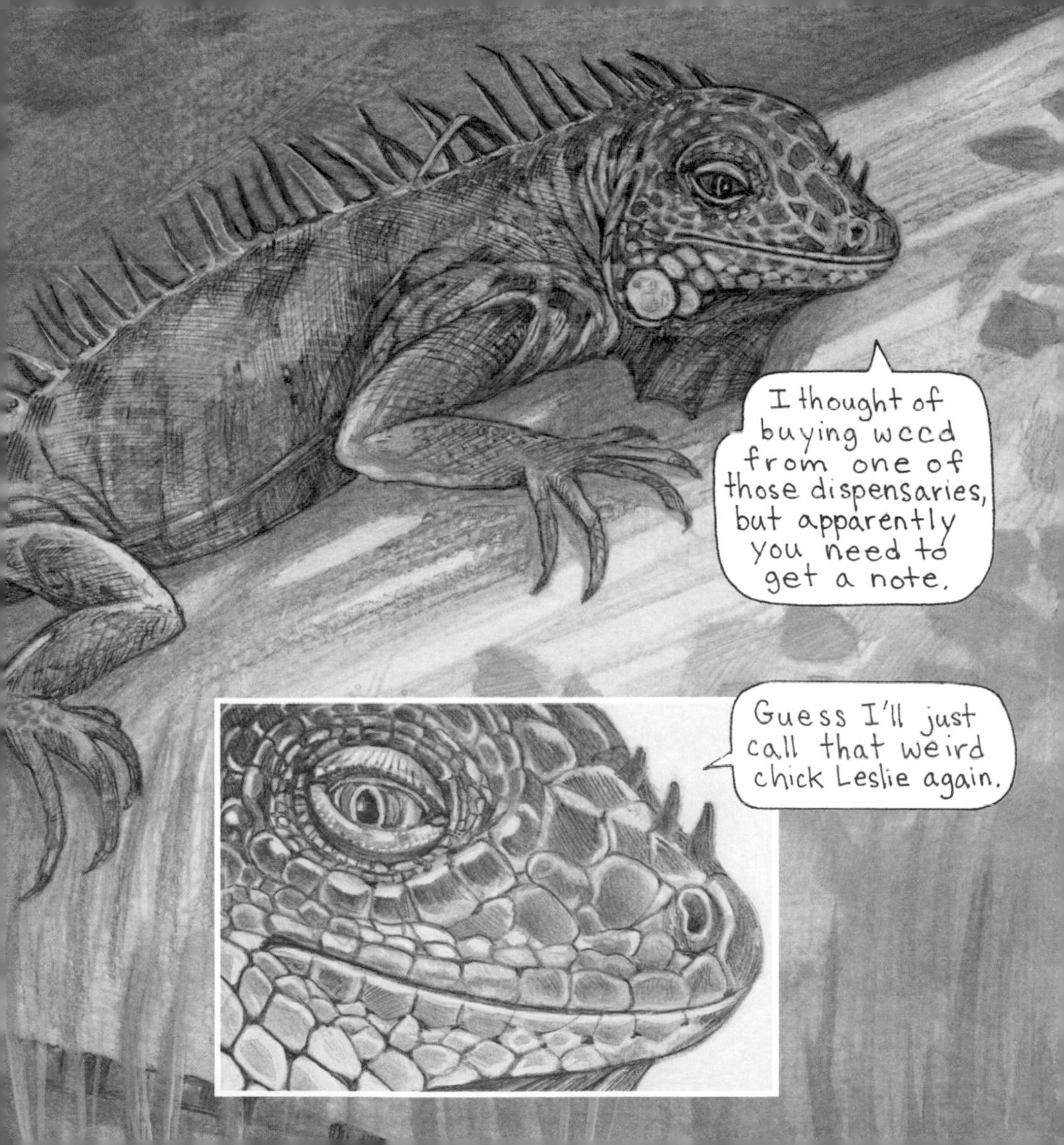
I thought of buying wccd from one of those dispensaries, but apparently you need to get a note.
Guess I'll just call that weird chick Leslie again.

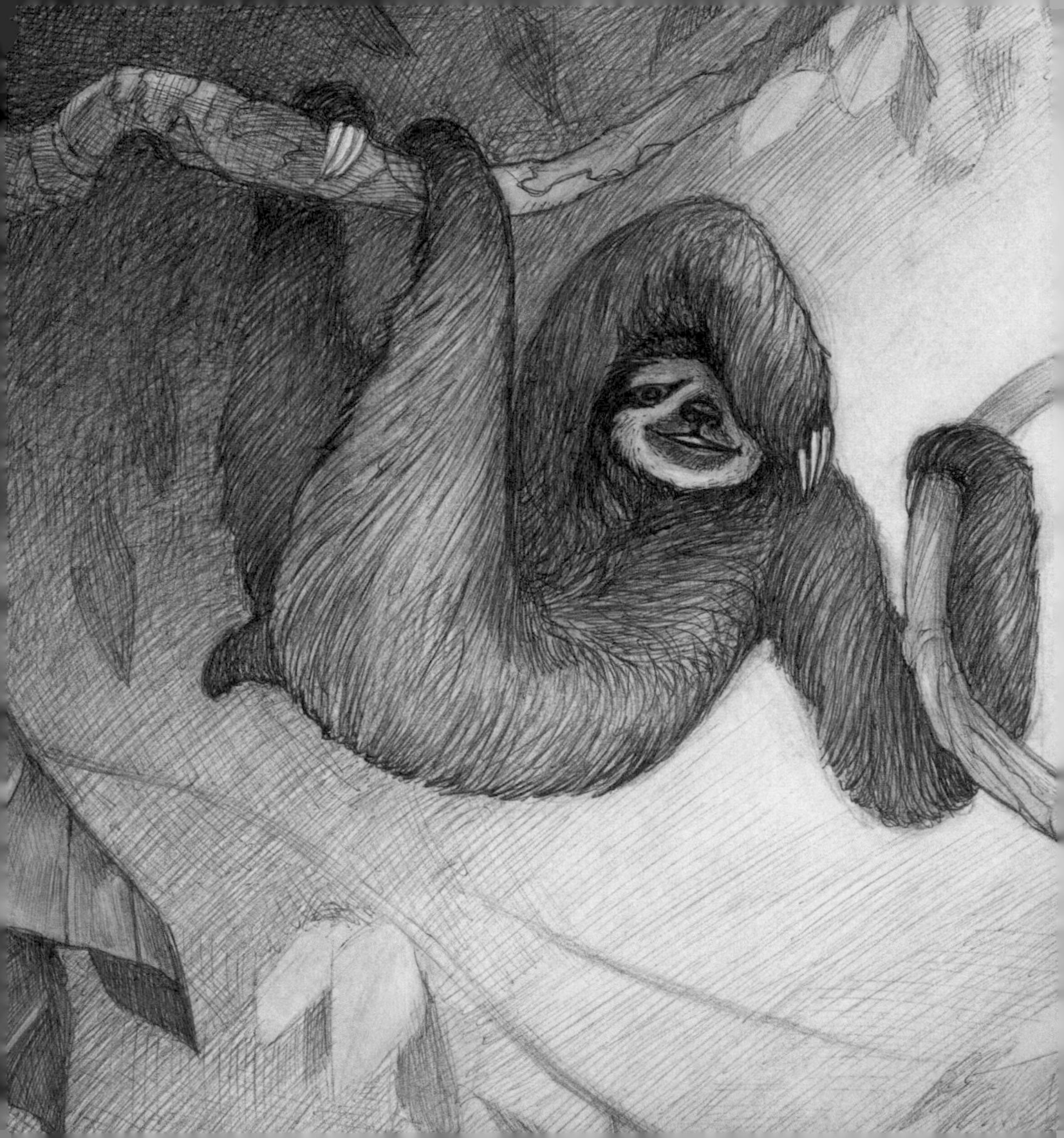

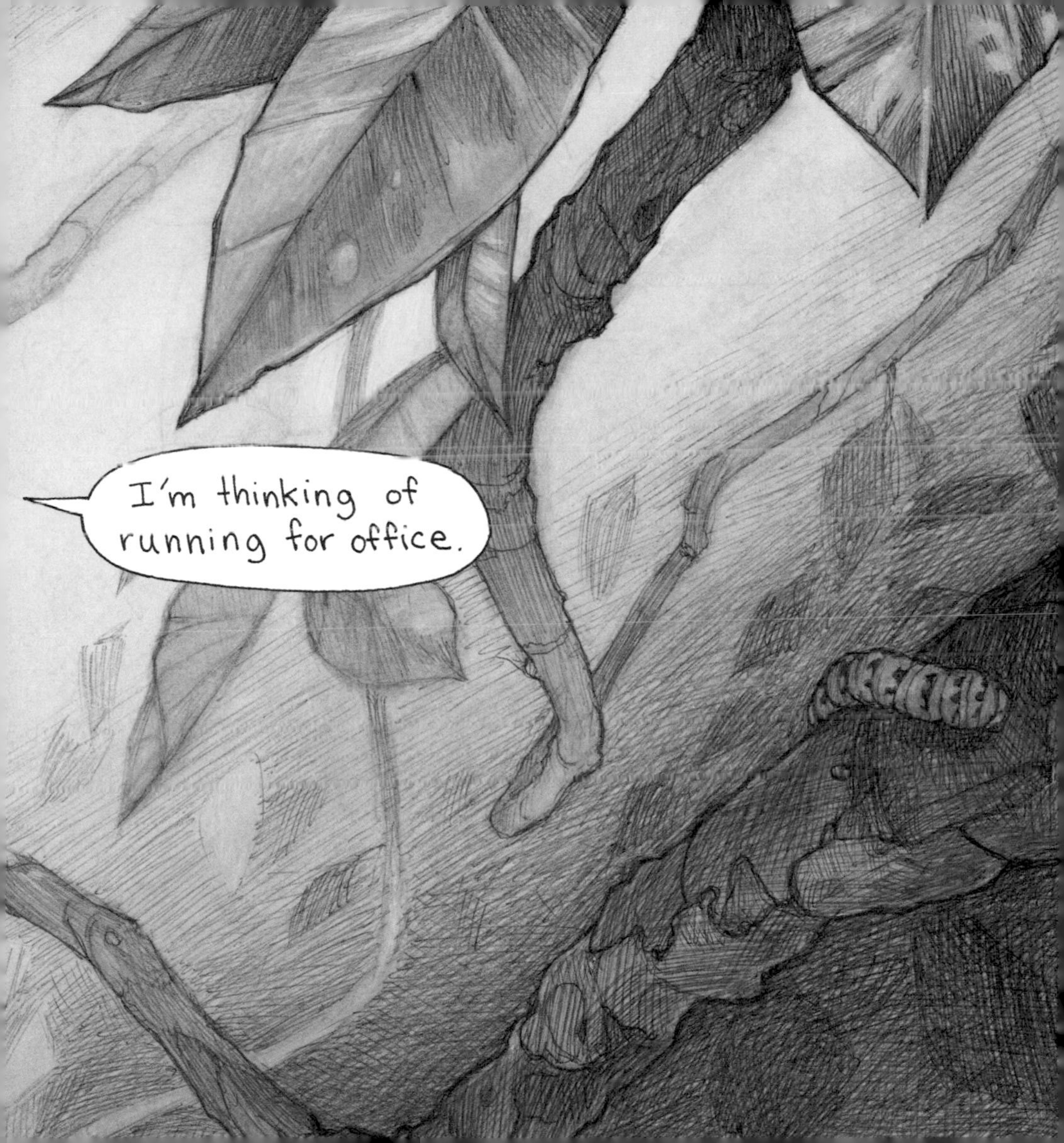
I'm thinking of running for office.

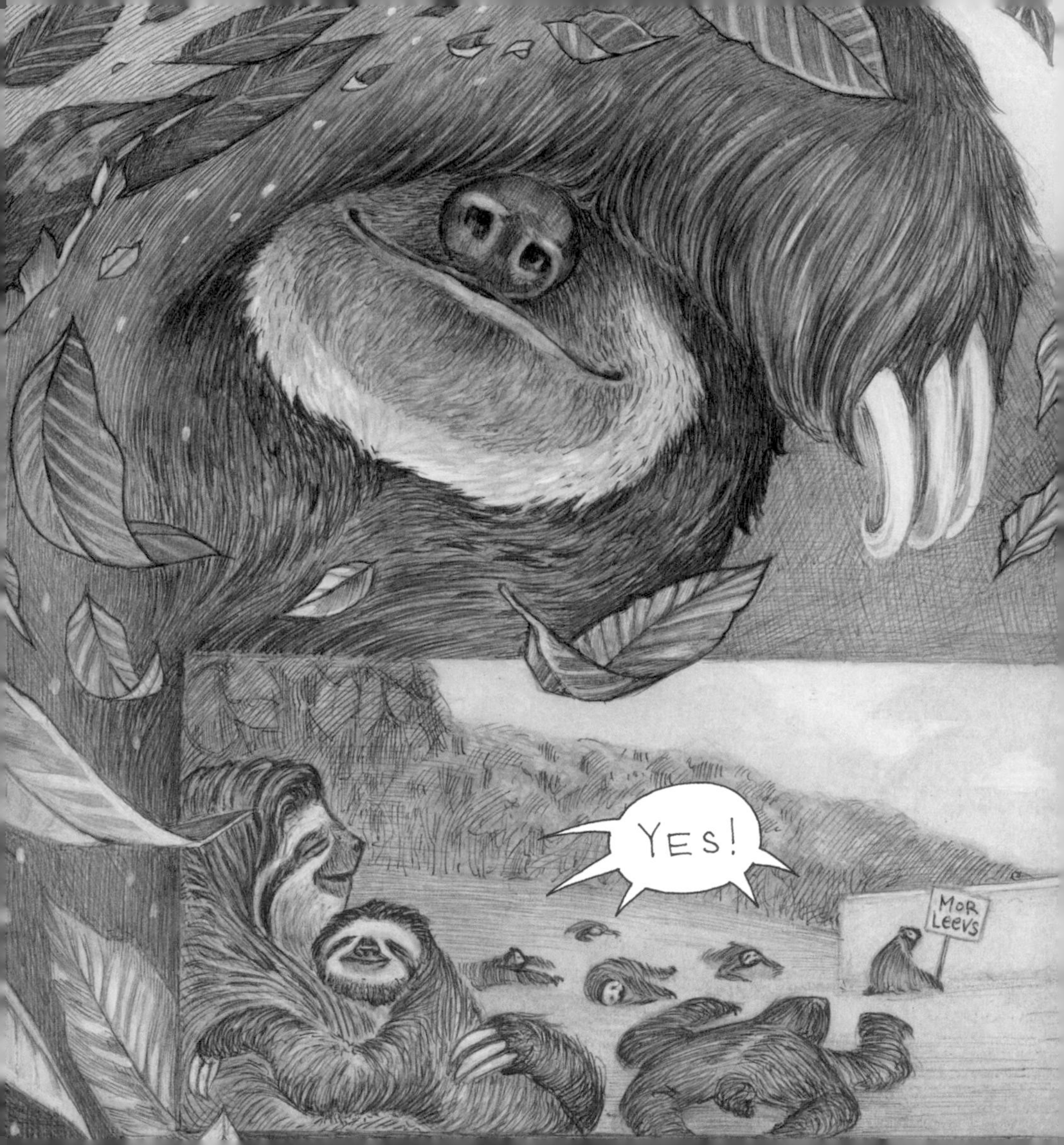
YES!
MOR LEEVS

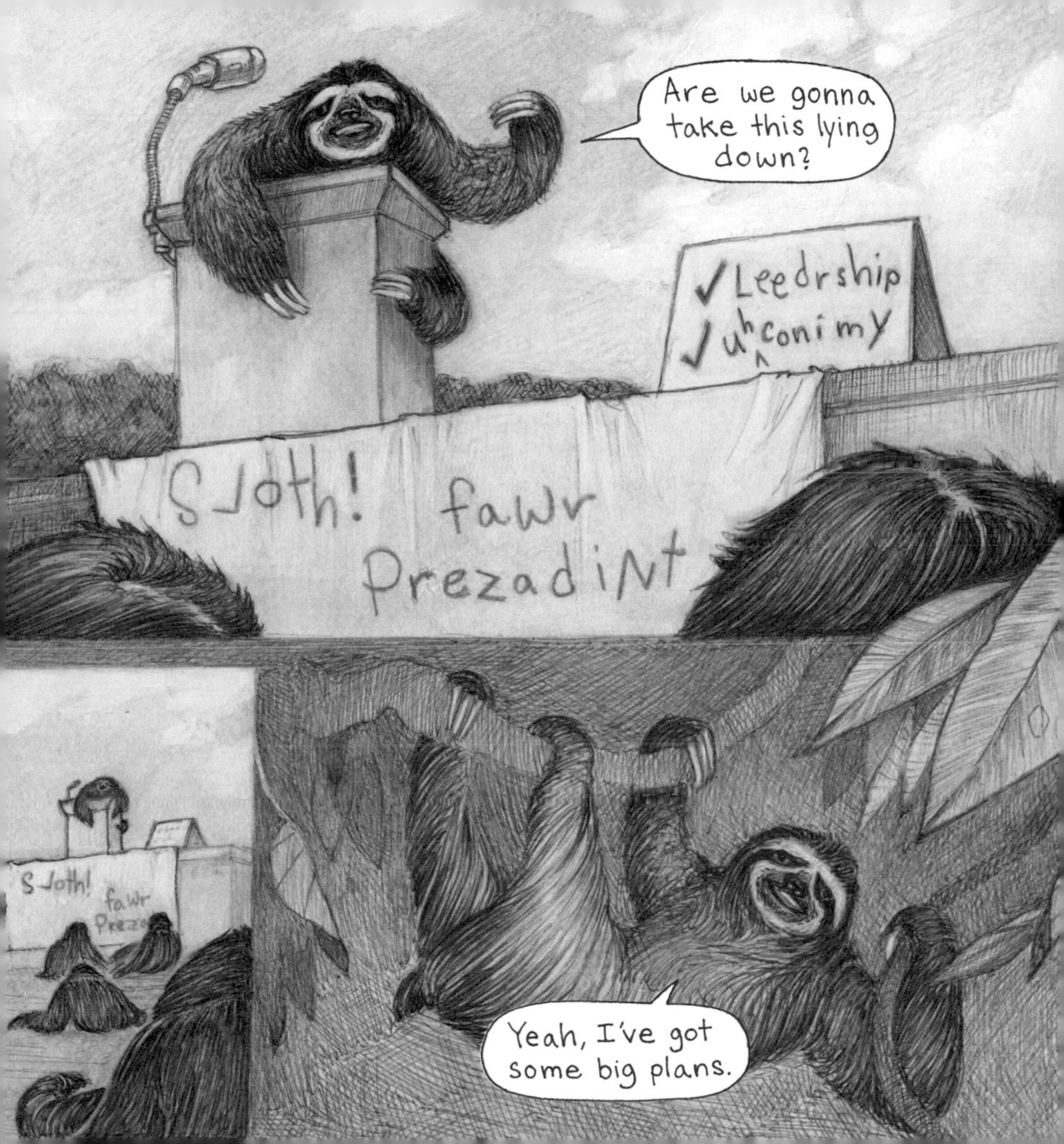
Are we gonna take this lying down?
✓Leedrship
✓uhconimy
Sloth! fawr Prezadint
Sloth! fawr Preza
Yeah, I've got some big plans.

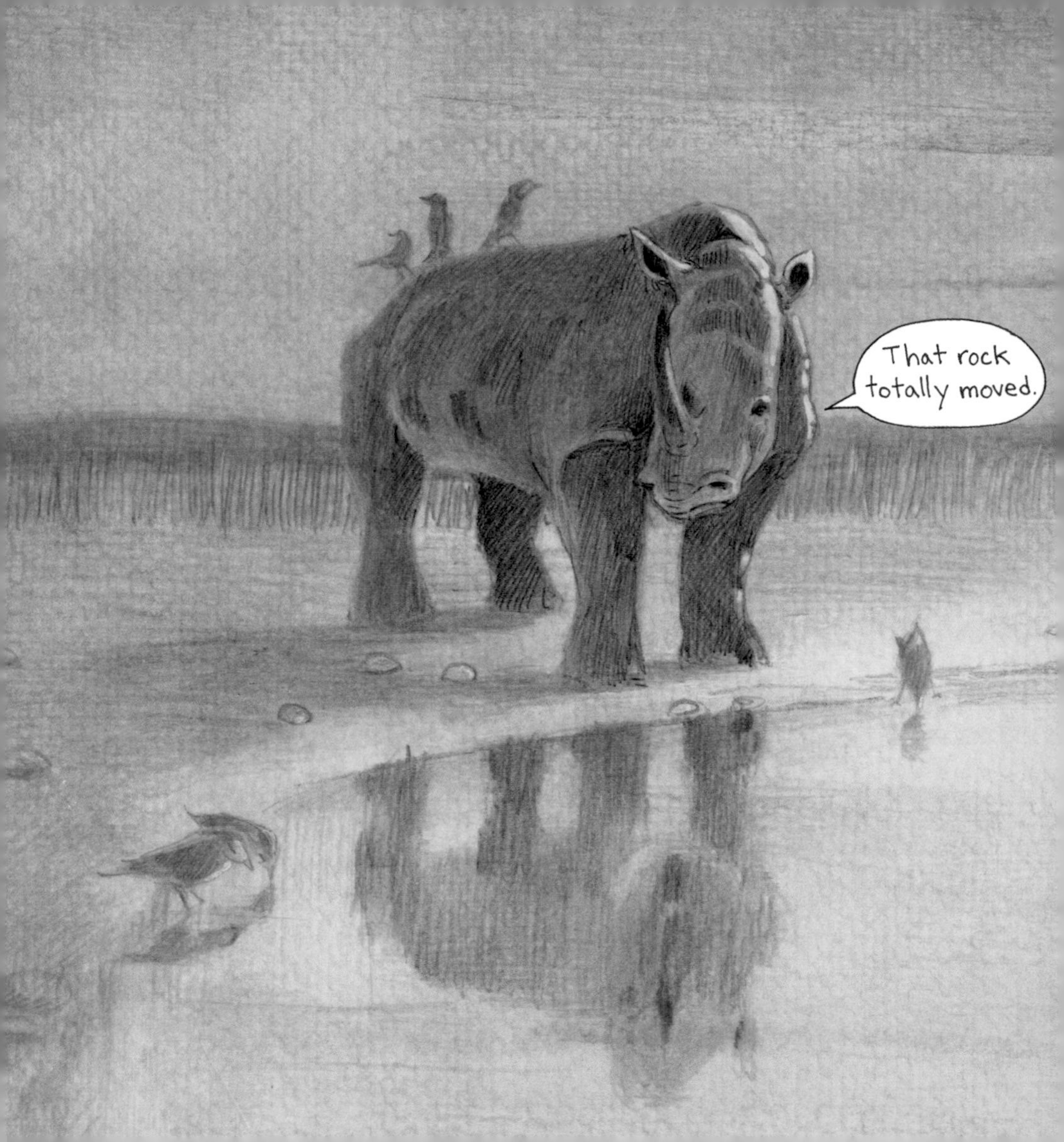
That rock totally moved.

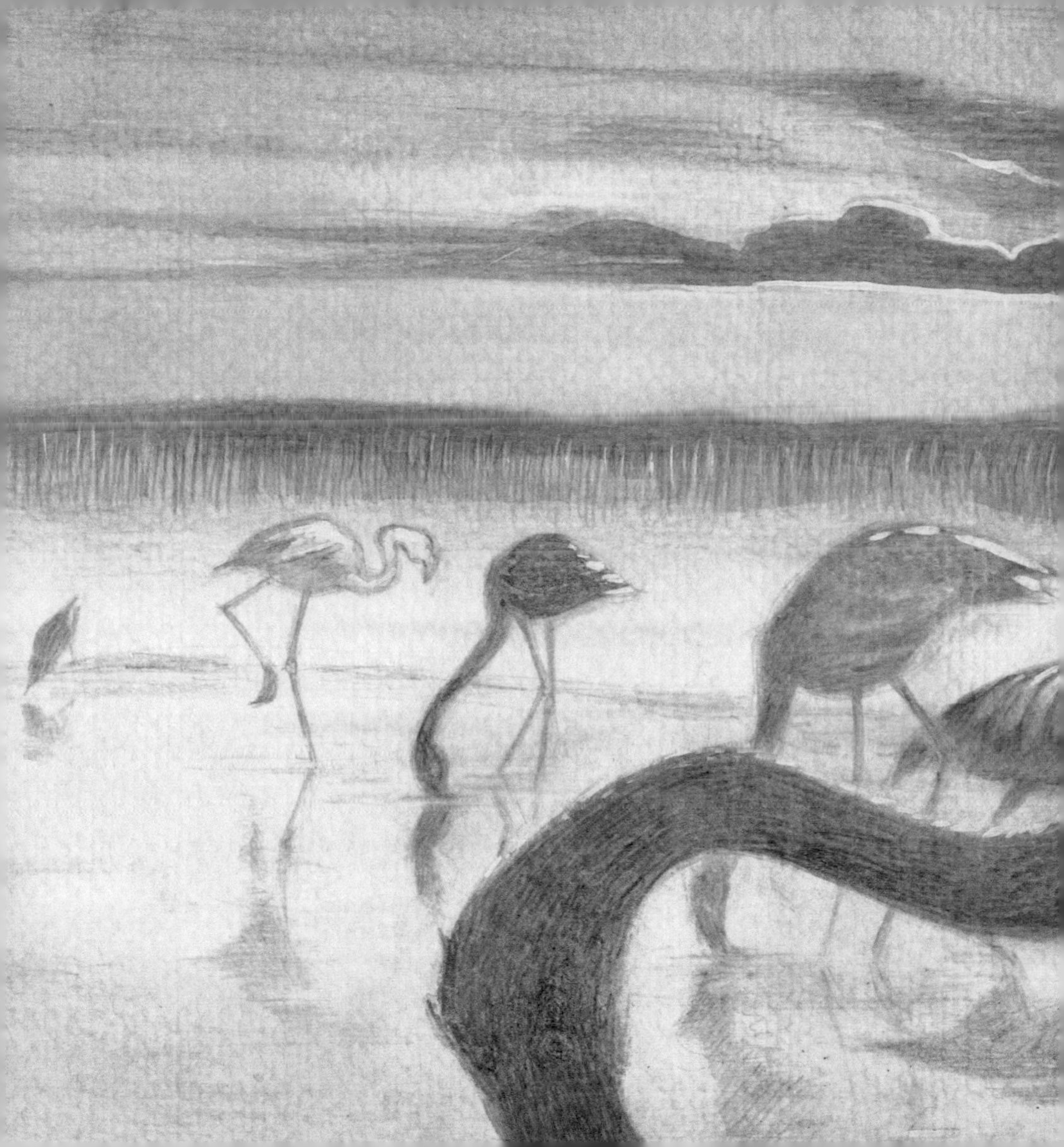

Acknowledgments

Many thanks to Steve Mockus, Neil Egan, and everyone at Chronicle Books. To my friends and family: Colin Burnett, Jim Anderson, Mom, Dad, and Herschel. And to all the animals, everywhere.

About the Author

Simon Winheld is an illustrator and an actor. He lives in New York City on a swivel chair.